PRINCIPLES OF COOKING IN WEST AFRICA

LEARN THE ART OF AFRICAN HERITAGE FOO FOO AND SOUP COOKING

BY

RAYMOND ESSANG

Bloomington, IN Milton Keynes, UK

authorHOUSE

AuthorHouse™
1663 Liberty Drive, Suite 200
Bloomington, IN 47403
www.authorhouse.com
Phone: 1-800-839-8640

AuthorHouse™ *UK Ltd.*
500 Avebury Boulevard
Central Milton Keynes, MK9 2BE
www.authorhouse.co.uk
Phone: 08001974150

First published by AuthorHouse 5/2/2006

ISBN: 1-4208-5996-X (sc)

Printed in the United States of America
Bloomington, Indiana

This book is printed on acid-free paper.

DEDICATED TO MY FATHER CHIEF H. O. ESSANG

TABLE OF CONTENTS

CHAPTER TWO

CHAPTER THREE

CHAPTER FOUR

CHAPTER SIX

ACKNOWLEDGEMENTS

This book would not have been written with success without the support of several people. Accordingly, I express my thanks and appreciation.

I thank my brothers Hon. Justice Essang, Major Ita Essang (rtd.) and his wife for their help in providing input.

I thank my father chief H.O.Essang a Methodist preacher who contributed tremendously through research work in making this book a reality. To him I dedicate this book as a token of my appreciation.

I thank my sisters Afiong, Nkoyo and Christina whose knowledge of cooking helped me develop skill through observation and emulation.

I also give thanks to Mr. Peter Archibong of Computer Technology Corporation, Atlanta who helped by providing the basic computer skills when this book was written on computer screen. Also Dr.Zakhiyya Thomas of the Atlanta University Center, and Mr. Phillip Ijoma who also helped in editing the manuscript. My sincere thanks also goes to Ms. Savonne Hill of American Express Company who assisted through words of encouragement.

And last but not the least, my late mother whose enormous ideas in preparation of varieties of African foods made me conceive this cook book. May her soul rest in peace.

Raymond Essang

INGREDIENTS FOR THIS COOK BOOK <u>RECIPE</u>S ARE AVAILABLE IN AFRICAN, INTERNATIONAL, ORIENTAL ,CARIBBEAN, TROPICAL, SPANISH OR ASIAN FOOD STORES. REFER TO YELLOW OR WHITE PAGES IN THE TELEPHONE BOOK UNDER GROCERS.

PREFACE

This book is written on African foods in order to educate the Americans and people all over the world about its secret. The goodness and excitement of this food are too great for me to bear alone . Due to lack of knowledge, people fail to realize that the corner stone of healthy living lies in the eating of food prepared naturally, devoid of chemicals and additives that deprive food of its values. Africans prepare their foods fresh. Canning and storing food too long destroy its values. For example, some food values like vitamin "C" could be destroyed easily by overcooking. Leafy fresh vegetables, like okra, spinach, green pepper, do not need much heat in their cooking.

African food is about the best in the world because it contains all the necessary essential ingredients, vitamins and minerals in one meal. For example, let us examine spinach okra soup eaten with foo foo like pounded yam ,amala or garri. Here, this soup and foo foo can nourish our body with all the necessary vitamins   like A,,B,C,D,E ---- --------Spinach okra soup contains the following ingredients as you are going to see in this cook book.

SPINACH or fluted pumpkin gives you vitamin A

OKRA gives vitamin B and A

FISH, MEAT gives vitamin B and D

PEPPER gives vitamin C as well as helping your stomach produce enough gastric juice for your digestion.

TOMATO gives vitamin C

PALM OIL gives vitamin E .and D

You can now be aware of obtaining all your vitamins in one meal, each time you eat foo foo.

Most Americans eat their full meal every day in the fast food restaurants. Some eat just chicken or hamburger without realizing that they only feed on protein from the only source –the chicken and no vitamins or minerals included in such a diet.   This is one of the reasons why a lot of people get sick.

In 1989 I met some Americans in Nigeria in West Africa. They were surprised that obesity was uncommon among the natives and that they looked strong and healthy.

African Americans like to eat soul food in most cases but African food is better.

Africans who live in the United States still eat their cultural foods.

African food is very nutritious and is among the best in the world. The method of preparation is very simple. All over Africa - from Senegal to Liberia, Ghana, Nigeria, Kenya, Ethiopia, Somalia, Tanzania, and South Africa, Africans prepare and eat their foods in the same style and manner. This is wonderful and natural. Various methods in which Africans cook their foods are elaborated in this book in a nutshell. Most of the recipes can be found in United States. However, the methods of preparation are African styles.

This book, is a threshold to fitness if you are health conscious and weight watchers. Buy it for yourself, friends, and loved ones and discover the root of your original heritage. Try our various stews, African snacks like akara, fresh fish, pounded yam, garri, moyin--moyin , ekoki , roasted or baked corn on the cob, various soups and snacks. It is the cultural food of your ancestors many years ago. Eat it, it will make you strong and healthy.

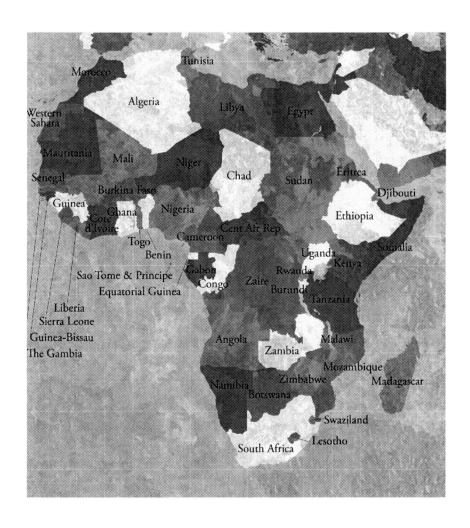

CHAPTER ONE
THE STAPLE FOODS

THE STAPLE FOODS

The principal staple foods consumed by most Africans are

Beans	Spices
Rice	Seeds
Cocoyam	Snails
Yam	Maize
Soya beans	Fish
Plantain	Chicken
Beni-seed	Onion
Bush	Meat
Wheat	Red pepper
Okra	Water leaves
Herbs	Guinea Corn
Eggs	
Tomatoes	Coconuts
Cassava or yuga root(manioc)	Vegetables

CHEMICAL FUNCTIONS OF POTASH

Potash is a compound of potassium and salt, a mineral found locally in nature. It is alkaline. It has the ability of neutralizing the acidity of food both in cooking and in the stomach. This is one of the reasons most Africans dissolve potash in water and drink when they have colic. Another function of potash is that of aiding in the formation of bile for the digestion of fats and oil to glycerol. When cooked with palm oil or vegetable oil, it emulsifies red palm oil to orange creamy product and vegetable oil to milky creamy product, hence neutralizing the effects of cholesterol in the African foods.

Potash acts as a solvent thus making fats easily digestible by the process of hydrolysis known as saponification. This reduces fats and oil to soap. The notion that oil and water don't mix does not apply to potash. It has the ability of blending and mixing oily soups like owo soup or otong soup together thus eliminating the effect of fat and oil deposit in the food.

The importance of African potash cannot be over emphasized in this book. Potash also helps in the development of teeth and bones. It is a very useful mineral intake for arthritis sufferers. Potash also acts as a catalyst in speeding up cooking time, especially in tough meat and leguminous fibers.

It is imperative you use the authentic ingredients as specified by the author in this cook book to prepare your palatable meal. They are all healthy foods.

PREPARATION OF FERMENTED AFRICAN OIL BEAN SEEDS

The African oil bean seeds are prepared using the following steps:

1. Boil the seeds of the African oil beans for approximately 90 minutes.
2. Peel the oil bean seeds.
3. Cut the seeds into slivered slices.
4. Mix the slivered seeds with potash and salt as needed.
5. Pick approximately 8 oz. of the slivered seeds and fold in a plantain leaf cut in approximate size of 5 x 8ins.
6. Place all folded slivered seeds near a heat source or sun for approximately one week to ferment. The seeds are then ready to be used for flavoring the soups.

METHODS OF PREPARATION

This depends on a individual's choice and taste. The commonest methods are (a) boiling (b) roasting (c) frying (d) steaming (e) stewing (f) baking and (g) grilling.

GARRI MANUFACTURING

Garri is one of the most important staple food. Garri is to Africans as bread is to Americans. It is prepared from cassava.

The period set side for its harvest after planting is one year. During this time, the cassava matures enough for reaping.

The cassava is uprooted from the ground, peeled, washed, and grated. The grated cassava is put into a strong porous bag and tied with a rope. Heavy weight is placed on the bag to ensure that its water content is completely squeezed out. It is allowed to remain for 3 days. The bag is then untied and sieved with a special filter to remove the chaffs and to enable it to sift like sand.

Garri pot is warm up on a stove. A few drops of palm oil may be added to facilitate frying and to give garri its characteristics light orange color. The sieved garri is fried a little at a time, stirring continuously with a wooden spatula. Continue stirring until garri is well fried and dried. The fried garri is now dry and crispy.

PREPARATION OF EBA

(cooked garri)

Eba is a name given to garri dough prepared by stirring garri thoroughly in boiled water. Depending on an individual's choice, it can be made hard or soft by using water accordingly. It can also be called garri foo foo and is eaten with soup.

SOAKED GARRI

Garri can be eaten by mixing with cold water. Some people prefer drinking it with salt or sugar. It can be eaten with dried fish or shrimps.

MANUFACTURING OF ORIGINAL FOO-FOO

(cassava foo foo)

Among Africans living in the United States, foo-foo is a general name given to any edible dough that can be eaten with soup. In West Africa, original foo-foo or cassava foo foo as it is some times called is prepared using almost the garri manufacturing method except that the squeezed grated cassava is not fried. But instead, it is soaked under water in a vessel for three days.

Put enough water and the squeezed grated cassava in a pot and cook. Stir continuously with a wooden spatula until a big ball of dough is formed.

In the United States, manufacturing of original foo foo for consumption is not necessary. Other pre-manufactured food items, like bisquick, farina, mashed potatoes, semolina or semovita can be substituted for the cassava or original foo-foo.

USING BISQUICK, SEMOLINA, , SEMOVITA OR FARINA AS FOO-FOO:

Put enough bisquick or any substitute into a pot of boiled water. Use enough water for consistency. Stir continously until dough is formed. If the dough is too soft add a little bisquick. If too hard, add water accordingly until you reach consistency . To prevent dough from sticking to the pot, smear a teaspoonful of butter or oil in the bottom of the pot. Be careful not to allow formation of lumps. Stir continuously until cooked.

This dough is called bisquick foo foo. If it were semolina it would be called semolina foo foo. It can be eaten or swallowed with soup. All varieties of foo-foo are eaten in the same manner of using hand, or spoon and fork.

With hand, wash your hands, mold the foo foo into a small ball of approximately an inch in diameter, dip in the soup and chew or swallow. With spoon cut enough foo foo, roll into a ball, pick with fork, dip into a bowl of soup and eat or swallow.

MANY WEIGHT WATCHERS PREFER USING FARINA, SEMOVITA, GARRI OR SEMOLINA BECAUSE THEY CONSIDER BISQUICK AND MASHED POTATOES TO BE FATTENING.

GENERAL PREPARATION OF YAM / POTATOES:

Yam can be prepared in different ways, depending on an individual's choice. It may be boiled and eaten with palm oil, pepper and salt or it may be cooked as pottage. Ingredients like vegetable oil, dried fish or meat are added.

Pottage can also be prepared with or without palm or vegetable oil. If palm or vegetable oil is not added then it is called " White Pottage."

Yam or potatoes can also be boiled and pounded. If pounded, it is called "Pounded yam". It is eaten with soup as foo foo.

Fried yam is another staple food for Africans. Yams can also be roasted in an oven and eaten with vegetable oil, cray fish, onions or boiled garden eggs.

In the United States, mashed potatoes can also be a substitute for pounded yam.

PREPARATION OF RICE:

Rice can be boiled and eaten with stew. It can be prepared by combining ingredients and also be made into dough and eaten as foo-foo like tuwo chinkafa.

PREPARATION OF COCO-YAM AND WATER-YAM.

Cocoyam and water yam have all the qualities and the usages of yams. They are prepared in similar manner.

Cocoyams and wateryams are peeled, grated and wrapped with young cocoyam leaves or spinach leaves. Palm oil is rubbed in the bottom of the pot to prevent the wrapped grated cocoyam from burning. A cut-off-tail periwinkle which is optional are evenly spread on the bottom of the pot. The palm oil rubbed in the bottom of the pot and the periwinkles are to prevent the wrapped grated cocoyams from burning.

This is explained in details in the preparation of ekpangnkukwo and ikokore.

PREPARATION OF CORN FOOD

Corn in Africa can be eaten in the following <u>methods</u>

(1) Boiling - boil fresh corn for approximately 20 minutes. Salt and butter may be added. It is eaten directly from the cob.

(2) Roasting - It can be roasted or baked in an oven and eaten with peanuts.

PREPARATION OF OGI

(corn starch)

Ogi is prepared from corn kernels.

(1) Soak corn kernels in water overnight.

(2) Drain out the water and grind in a blender.

(3) Mix with plenty of water and filter with a fine sieve.

(4) Keep the sieved liquid overnight for the starch to settle.

(5) Replace the water with fresh water, just enough to cover the starch. Store in a refrigerator. This is ogi and it is used in the preparation of akamu.

EKPANG NKPONG OR ANYAN EKPANG

(wrapped grated cocoyam pie)

serves 4

RECIPE:

Coco yams   3 lbs

Salt ---   2 tablespoonfuls

METHOD:

(1) Peel cocoyams properly and grate in the same manner, that cassava is grated.

(2) Add two tablespoonfuls of salt and mix thoroughly.

(3) Cut plantain leaves into small rectangular sizes of approximately 6" by 10" and warm both ends in flame to facilitate wrapping or use aluminum foil in similar manner.

(4) Rub oil on each leaf or foil that is to be used. Scoop approximately two tablespoonfuls of the grated coco yam and properly wrap it with either the plantain leaf or foil in the form of a pie or to form a pie.

(5) Cut four pieces of the plantain leaf mid-rib into approximate length of 6 inches each to serve as a layer or pallet in the bottom of the pot. (If aluminum foil is used as a substitute, then use equivalent length of sticks as a layer) or just leave it like that without placing layer.

(6) Arrange the wrapped grated coco yam pies on the layer in the pot. Add a little water and boil for 20 minutes in steam. This is to enable the wrapped grated cocoyam to harden. Continue this process of adding little water and boiling in steam for additional 90 more minutes. Ekpang is now ready to be served.

Best served with otong or abak soup.

EKPANG IWA

(wrapped grated cassava pie)

special food for Oron people

serves 3

RECIPE

Cassava – grated -----4 lbs.

METHOD:

(1)Peel cassava.

(2)Cut into two or three pieces.

(3)Grate in a grater.

(4)Mix properly with a little water.

(5)Shape aluminum foil into small bags of approximately 4" by 6" in dimension or use the plantain leaf cut into approximate size of 5" by 10". Soften both ends of each leaf by warming in flame to facilitate wrapping.

(6)Rub oil on each leaf or foil that is to be used. Scoop approximately two tablespoonfuls of the grated cassava and carefully wrap it using either the plantain leaf or aluminum foil.

(7) Cut approximately six 4 inch piece of plantain or banana leaf mid-rib or equivalent pieces of any stick to serve as a layer pallet in a pot.

(8) Arrange the wrapped grated cassava pies on the layer and boil in steam in the similar manner as previously did with wrapped grated cocoyam pies. Boil for 90 minutes.

Best served with otong or palm-fruit-cream soup or banga soup.

ROASTED COCO YAM

This is baked in an oven. When ready, it can be served with palm oil and salt.

FRIED COCO YAM, YAM OR POTATOES

Peel cocoyams, yams or potatoes and slice them into little pieces. Fry in a vegetable oil. Served with palm oil, meat or fish.

USUNG

(pounded cocoyam)

Same as pounded yam both are prepared using similar method.

SOMETHING TO REMEMBER

Drink plenty of water after each meal. When using palm oil, use pure red liquid type because that is the best quality palm oil. Do not use a thick orange type. Cut-off-tail periwinkles are eaten by sucking the meat. This is a very good source of calcium. ALSO NOTE THAT MOST INGREDIENTS IN THIS COOK BOOK ARE AVAILABLE IN AFRICAN, INTERNATIONAL, ORIENTAL, CARIBBEAN, TROPICAL, SPANISH OR ASIAN FOOD STORES. REFER TO YELLOW OR WHITE PAGES IN THE TELEPHONE BOOK UNDER GROCERS.

BANGA PREPARATION

(Palm-fruit cream)

PREPARATION OF PALM-FRUIT CREAM

(1)Wash approximately 3 lbs. of palm fruits and boil.

(2)Filter out the water and beat it in a mortar until the soft succulent pulp separates from the nuts.

(3)Pour it into clean boiled 3/4 gallon of water and mix to a proper consistency.

(4)Filter out the palm fruit pulp from its residue. The cream is now ready to be used for cooking various palm-fruit-cream soups.

PREPARATION OF COCONUT MILK

(1)Break a coconut and carve it out from its shell.

(2) Wash and grate finely.

(3) Put the grated nut in a container and add a little warm water.

(4) Filter out the milk with a fine sieve. Add more water to make sure that the milk is completely filtered.

Alternatively, you can purchase a processed canned coconut milk in your nearest African food store.

IYAN

(yam flour)

(1) Peel about 6 lbs of yam and slice it into very thin pieces. Allow it to dry properly in the sun or any heat source. This takes two to three days if using sun. Grind in a mill.

The yam flour is now ready. In the United States, already processed yam flour is available in African food stores.

PREPARATION OF AMALA

Amala is a name given to yam foo-foo. It is prepared by using yam flour. Boil about 1 quart of water in a pot. Add the yam flour as needed to form a soft dough. Continue stirring for about 10-mins until properly converted to a smooth dough.

Amala is served with okra or ewedu soup.

CHAPTER TWO
PLANTAIN FOODS

IWUK UKOM

(plantain pottage)

serves 4

RECIPE:

Plantains -- green -- chopped	6 large
Palm oil or vegetable oil	1/4 pts.
Salt and pepper	to taste
Fresh tomatoes -- chopped	3-medium
Tomato paste -- small	1/2 tin
Cray fish -- ground	1 oz.
Dried fish -- cut into pieces	2 lbs.
Maggi cube or accent	4 cubes
Onion	1 medium

METHOD:

(1) Peel plantains and chop them in small pieces.

(2) Add the prepared tomatoes, onion, pepper, maggi cubes, salt, fish and cray fish to a pot of approximately one quart of water and cook.

(3) While boiling, add the chopped plantains and stir. Cook for 15 minutes.

(4) Add oil, reduce heat and allow to simmer for 5-minutes. It is now ready to be served as a complete meal.

PLANTAIN AND BEAN POTTAGE

serves 4

RECIPE

Plantains -- little chunks	5 plantains
Beans -- black eyed pea	2 lbs
Palm oil	1/4 pint
Cray fish -- ground	1 oz
Salt and pepper	as needed
Dried fish	2 medium
Tomatoes -- fresh - chopped	3 medium
Onions -- chopped	2 medium

METHOD

1. Boil beans until soft.

2. Peel plantains and cut into little chunks.

3. In a pot containing the soft boiled beans, add cray fish, salt and pepper as needed, dried fish or meat, fresh tomatoes, onions and the plantains. Boil and stir gently.

4. Cook for 15 minutes. Add palm oil and simmer for 5 minutes.

   Serve as a complete meal.

SPINACH PLANTAIN POTTAGE

Serves 3

RECIPE

Unripe plantains -- chunks	6 plantains
Spinach -- chopped	1 lb
Cray fish -- ground	1 oz
Meat	3 lbs
Palm oil	1/4 pint
Onions -- chopped	2 medium
Salt and pepper	as needed
Maggi cube	4 cubes
Stock fish	8 pieces

METHOD:

1. Peel plaintains and wash.

2. Into a pot containing one pint of water, put the following ingredients; crayfish, onions, fish or meat, maggi cubes, salt and pepper as needed. Cook.

3. As soon as it starts boiling, add the plantains and spinach, then palm oil. Stir gently with a wooden spoon. Cook for 15 minutes.

4. Simmer for 5 minutes.

   Serve as a complete meal.

SPINACH PLANTAIN PALM FRUIT CREAM POTTAGE

The recipe is similar to that of spinach plantain pottage except that palm fruit cream is used instead of palm oil.

YAM PALM FRUIT CREAM POTTAGE

serves 5

RECIPE

Palm fruit cream	1 can
Yam or potatoes	3 lbs
Onions	2 medium
Salt and pepper	as needed
Meat or dried fish	2 lbs
Cray fish	1 oz
Stock fish	8 pieces
Maggi or accent	as needed

METHOD

1. Peel yam or potatoes and cut into chunks.
2. Put the yam chunks or potatoes into a pot containing approximately one pint of water.
3. Add crayfish, onions, meat ,fish, stock fish and magi cubes salt and pepper as needed.
4. After boiling add palm fruit cream. Cook for 10 minutes.
5. Allow to simmer for 5 minutes.

Serve as a complete meal.

YAM SPINACH PALM FRUIT CREAM POTTAGE

The recipe is similar to that of the potatoes or the yam palm fruit cream pottage, except that spinach is added when adding yam.

DODO

(ripe plantain chips)

serves 4

RECIPE:

Ripe plantains	8 large
Salt	as needed
Ground red pepper	as needed
Vegetable oil	1 pt.

METHOD:

(1) Wash and peel ripe plantains.

(2) Slice them into pieces .

(3) Sprinkle with salt.

(4) Heat vegetable oil until hot and fry till they turn brownish.

Best served with fresh milk or soft drink for breakfast.

GREEN PLANTAIN CHIPS

serves 4

RECIPE:

Green plantains or green bananas	8 large
Salt	as needed
Vegetable oil	as needed

METHOD:

(1)Wash and peel green bananas.

(2)Slice them into pieces.

(3)Sprinkle with salt.

(4)Heat the vegetable oil until hot and fry little slices at a time until they turn brownish.

Serve with fresh milk or any beverage for break fast.

BOLI

(roasted plantain)

(1)Carefully peel the plantain .

(3)Put into the oven and bake until done.

Boli is now ready and can be served with coconut or roasted peanuts.

CHAPTER THREE
PREPARATION OF RICE FOODS

CHICKEN JOLLOF RICE

serves 5

<u>RECIPE:</u>

Hen -- boiled and cut	3 lbs.
Rice	3 lbs
Fresh tomatoes -- chopped	2 medium
Tomato paste -- small	1/2 can
Fresh red pepper and salt	as needed
Onions -- sliced -- ground	2-medium
Vegetable oil	1/4 pt.
Boullion cubes	4 cubes
Cray fish - ground	1 oz

<u>METHOD</u>

(1) Grind one fresh onion, and slice the other. Slice one fresh tomato and grind the other.

(2) In a pot of water, add ground tomatoes, ground onion, rice, boiled hen, bouillon cubes, and crayfish. Bring the content to boil. Add oil. Just before the rice is about to become soft, spread the sliced onions and tomatoes on the rice. Allow to simmer until water dries off.

Can be served with banana for dinner.

SHRIMP COCONUT RICE

serves 4

RECIPE:

Rice	3 lbs
Shrimps -- shelled	2 lbs
Coconut milk - 2 cans or	3/4 gallon (prepared)
Salt and pepper	as needed
Onion -- 1/2 sliced,	1/2 ground 1 large
Boullion cubes	4 cubes
Cray fish -- ground	1 oz
Tomatoes -- fresh	2 large

METHOD:

(1) Prepare coconut milk or buy the processed one in African food store.

(2) Shell shrimps and split into two portions Grind 1/2 onion and tomato and slice the other half.

(3) In a pot containing the coconut milk or approximately 1 quart of water mixed with 2 cans of coconut milk, add ground onion, ground tomato, magi or bouillon cubes, ground crayfish, one portion shrimps, salt and pepper as needed. Bring the content to boil then add rice.

(4) When the rice is about to soften, spread the other portion of the shelled shrimps, the sliced onion, and tomato on the rice. Cook in steam. Allow to simmer. Add more coconut milk if necessary. Turn off heat.

It is now ready to be served.

SHRIMP JOLLOF RICE

serves 4

RECIPE:

Rice	3 lbs.
Shrimps -- shelled	2 lbs.
Fresh tomatoes - chopped	2 large
Onions -- chopped	2 large
Salt and ground pepper	as needed
Vegetable oil or palm oil	1/4 pt.
Magi cubes	3 cubes
Cray fish -- ground	1 oz.
Tomato paste -- small	1 tin

METHOD:

(1) Chop two fresh tomatoes and split into two portions.

(2) Chop two onions and split into two portions.

(3) Shell shrimps and split into two portions.

(4) Heat oil until smoked. Add one portion of the chopped onion and tomato and fry for 1 minute.

(5) Add water, rice, crayfish, tomato paste, one half of the shelled shrimps, pepper and salt as needed. Stir and allow to cook for 35-minutes.

(6) Before the rice softens, spread the other half of the salted shelled shrimps, sliced onion and tomato on the rice.

Add oil and let it cook in steam. Simmer for 10 minutes.
Serve with dodo, akara, banana or as a complete meal.

BEEF JOLLOF RICE

serves 5

RECIPE:

Meat—beef	3 lbs.
Rice	3 lbs.
Fresh tomatoes	2 medium
Tomato paste -- small	1/2 tin
Fresh red pepper & salt	as needed
Onion – chopped	1 medium
Vegetable oil or palm oil	1/4 pt.
Boullion cubes -- maggi cubes	4 cubes

METHOD:

(1) Cut meat into desirable small pieces and boil until tender.

(2) Chop onions, fresh tomatoes and fresh red pepper into small pieces.

(3) Add rice and all ingredients except oil. Cook with enough water as necessary.

(4) When the rice is about to become soft, add oil and simmer until the rice softens.

Serve as dinner or super.

PLAIN JOLLOF RICE

serves 5

<u>RECIPE</u>:

Rice	3 lbs.
Tomato paste -- small	1/2 can
Salt and fresh red pepper	as needed
Oregano	as needed
Fresh tomatoes -- chopped	2 medium
Vegetable oil	1/4 pt.
Dried fish -- cut	1 large
Shrimps -- shelled	1 lb.
Cray fish -- ground	1 oz.
Maggi cubes -- optional	2 cubes
Onions -- chopped	2 large

<u>METHOD</u>:

(1) Chop onion, fresh tomatoes and red pepper.

(2) Into a pot of water, add fish, shrimps, cray fish, maggi cubes and tomato paste and bring to boil.

(3) Add rice and stir gently. Add pepper and oregano as needed. Cook until the rice becomes almost soft, then add oil.

(4) Simmer for 10 minutes. The rice is now soft.

Can be served with banana.

AFRICAN FRIED RICE

FIRST <u>METHOD</u>

AFRICAN SHRIMP FRIED RICE

serves 4

<u>RECIPE</u>

Boiled rice -- uncle Ben's	3 lbs
Vegetable oil	1 pt
Shrimps -- shelled	2 lbs
Nutmeg or curry powder	as needed
Onion -- chopped	1 medium
Salt and pepper	to taste
Bell pepper -- chopped	1 pepper
Bullion cube or accent	as needed

<u>METHOD</u>

1. Put a little oil into frying pan and heat until smokes. Fry onions for approximately 30 seconds.
2. Sift the boiled rice into the pan. Stir continuously.
3. Add shelled shrimps, curry or nutmeg, pepper and salt and cook for 10 mins.
4. When the rice is almost becoming brownish, turn off the heat. Serve as a complete meal.

SECOND METHOD

1. Heat a little oil in a pan until smokes.
2. Put the rice in the oil and fry until brown ,preferably long grain rice like uncle Ben's. Continue stirring until the rice

changes to white or golden color. Then add a little water and continue boiling for 20 mins.

3. Add all the above ingredients and stir except the shrimp.

When you are about to put down the pot, put the shrimps, and let it simmer for 3 minutes.

Serve as a complete meal.

BEEF FRIED RICE

serves 4

RECIPE

Rice -- uncle ben's	3 lbs
Vegetable oil	1 pt
Beef -- chunks	1 lb
Pepper, salt ,nutmeg or curry --	as needed
Onion -- chopped	1 onion

METHOD

Heat the oil in a pot until smoke then fry the rice in the pot until golden brown.

1. Have a good portion of beef boiled with salt and very little water added and add it to the rice. Add onions. Add beef, curry or nutmeg, salt and pepper as needed.
2. Stir. Fry for 15 minutes, until water dries off.

Stir continuously for approximately 5 more minutes. Turn off the heat.

Serve hot or cold as a complete meal.

TUWO SHINKAFA

(rice foo-foo)

Serves 3

RECIPE:

1. Rice	5 lbs
2. Salt	to taste

METHOD:

(1)Put rice in a pot and boil until it softens. Add salt as needed.

(2)With the aid of a wooden spoon, mash the rice or pound it in a mortar.

Serve with any soup or stew.

CHAPTER FOUR
CORN, YAM AND COCOYAM FOODS

AKAMU

(corn starch or pap)

serves 3

RECIPE:

Ogi -- corn starch	1 lb.
Sugar	as needed

METHOD:

(1) Mix corn starch in a bowl with approximately 1/4 cup of water and sugar as needed.

(2) While stirring, pour in enough boiled water until corn starch thickens. Stir to a smooth paste. If not properly done, you can boil it on the stove.

This is akamu and it can be served with akara or moyin-miyin.

EKOKI

(corn pie)

serves 4

RECIPE:

Fresh corn --ground	3 lbs.
Palm oil or vegetable oil	1/4 pt.
Shrimps	1 lb.
Onion -- chopped	1 medium
Fresh red pepper	as needed
Boiled sliced eggs	3 eggs

Cray fish   1 oz.

METHOD:

(1) Mix together all the above ingredients with the ground fresh corn.

(2) Using either plantain leaves, banana leaves or aluminum foil cut in small rectangular shapes of approximately 6 by 10 inches. Rub oil on the inner side of the leaf or foil. Carefully wrap in small portions so as to form a pie.

(3) Place any small sticks to act as a pallet at the bottom of the pot, or no stick at all.

(4) Neatly arrange and place the wrapped pies on these sticks. First add a little water to enable the pies to harden in steam. Then put a little more water and cook for an hour.

Can be served with any beverage or fresh milk.

EFERE IBOKPOT

(corn meal)

serves 5

RECIPE:

Fresh corn -- kernels	3 lbs.
Palm oil or vegetable oil	1/4 pt.
Shrimps -- shelled	1 lb.
Cray fish -- ground	1 oz.
Fresh pepper	as needed

Salt   as needed

Fish or meat   2 lbs.

METHOD:

(1)Put all ingredients in a pot containing one quart of water
and cook for approximately 20-minutes.

Serve as a complete meal.

OTO IBOKPOT

(corn pudding)

serves 4

RECIPE:

Same as corn meal.

METHOD:

(1)Properly grind fresh corn kernels in a blender.

(2)Put all ingredients in a pot except the ground corn. Cook
with approximately one quart of water or add water as
needed.

(3)While boiling, sprinkle the fresh ground corn, a little at a
time. Stir continuously.

(4)Add palm oil and continue stirring for approximately 10
minutes.

Serve with any beverage, fruit juice or milk.

Old fashion method / ANYAN EKPANG

(boiled grated cocoyam pie)

serves 5

RECIPE:

Wateryam or cocoyam	6 lbs.
Salt	as needed
Plantain leaf or aluminum foil	

METHOD:

(1) Peel wateryam or cocoyam and grate with a blender.

(2) Mix with a little salt.

(3) Shape aluminum foil into small bags of about 6 by 10 inches, or plantain leaf cut into the size of 6 by 8 inches. Soften both ends of the leaf by warming in flame.

(4) Use same method of wrapping and arrangement as with ekoki.

(5) Allow to boil in steam for 80 minutes or until cooked. Best served with otong or banga soup.

New fashion / ASARO

(yam pottage)

serves 5

RECIPE:

Yams or potatoes	3 lbs
Onion -- sliced	1 large
Pepper -- red -- ground	as needed

Salt	as needed
Tomatoes -- sliced	two large
Palm oil or vegetable oil	1/4 pint
Dried fish	2 lbs.
Cray fish	1 oz.
Magi cubes or accent	as needed

METHOD:

(1) Peel yams or potatoes and cut them into pieces.

(2) In a pot of approximately 2 quarts of water, add sliced onion, crayfish, dried fish, ground pepper tomatoes and bring the content to boil.

(3) Before the potatoes or yams soften, add palm oil and simmer for 10-mins. Stir continuously until it turns paste.

This can be served for lunch or dinner.

POTATO AND BEAN POTTAGE

serves 4

RECIPE

Potatoes or yams	3 lbs
Beans -- black eyed peas	2 lbs
Cray fish	1/2 oz
Palm oil	1/4 pint
Meat or dried fish -- chunks	2 lbs
Onions	2 medium

Salt and pepper   as needed

Tomatoes -- fresh -- chopped   3 medium

METHOD

1. Boil black eyed pea beans until soft.

2. Peel yams or potatoes and cut into little chunks.

3. In a pot containing the soft boiled beans, put approximately 1 1/2 pints of water, crayfish, boiled meat, fresh tomatoes, onions and the chunky potatoes or yams, salt and pepper as needed. Stir with a wooden spoon.

4. Allow it to cook for 15 minutes, then simmer in a low heat for 5 minutes.

Turn off the heat and serve hot or cold.

IKOKORE

(wateryam ball pottage)

serves 4

RECIPE:

Water yams -- grated	3 lbs.
Onion -- chopped	1 medium
Cray fish -- ground	1 oz.
Salt	as needed
Pepper	as needed
Dried fish -- chopped	1 large
Shrimps -- shelled	1 lb.

METHOD:

(1) Peel and grate the water yams with a grater or blender.

(2) Boil approximately 2 quarts of water in a pot and put in all ingredients except the grated water yam.

(4) While the content is boiling cut bits of the grated water yam in small balls of approximately one inch in diameter. Carefully arrange them in the pot. Do not stir. When the content boils and the balls harden, then stir.

(5) At reduced heat, simmer for 10 minutes.

Serve as a complete meal.

Note that no vegetable oil is added in this particular food.

EKPANG NKUKWO

(grated cocoyam pottage)

serves 6

RECIPE:

Cocoyam or water yams or both mixed	4 lbs.
Shelled Periwinkles -- optional	1 lb.
Pepper -- ground	to taste
Salt -- accent	to taste
Palm oil	1/4 pint
Dried fish	I large
Cray fish -- ground	1 oz.

Spinach -- whole leaf or young cocoyam leaf.

This food is very nutritious and high in carbohydrates.

METHOD:

(1)Peel and grate cocoyam or water yams and mix them to a proper consistency.

(2)Cut the young cocoyam leaves in sizes of approximately 4 x 3 inches in this aspect use whole spinach leaf for wrapping.

(3)Grease the inside bottom of the pot by rubbing with palm oil. Spread in the cut off-tail-periwinkles. This method prevents the pot from burning. Uniformly place the wrapped grated cocoyams on the periwinkles. Remember, periwinkle is optional.

(4)With leaf on left fingers, scoop approximately one half teaspoonful of grated cocoyam and place on the leaf and roll up in a form of like a small tube-like finger using both thumb and fingers in wrapping. Arrange the rolled-up grated coco yams in an orderly fashion inside the pot. Continue this process until the grated cocoyam is all rolled up with the leaves. You might end up wrapping approximately 100 wrapped grated cocoyam like small pies.

(5)In the pot gently put a little quantity of water to enable the wrapped grated cocoyams pies to harden in steam before stirring. Cook for approximately 15 minutes. Then add a little more water as needed.

(6)Put the ground crayfish, fish, pepper, salt, etc. Cook for 30 mins.

(7)Add more water and stir gently with wodden spoon.

(8)Add palm oil, lower the heat and allow to simmer for 10 minutes.

Serve hot or cold as a meal.

ASA IWA

(grated cassava pottage)

serves 4

RECIPE:

Cassava	4 lbs.
Shelled periwinkles - optional	2 lbs
Pepper -- ground	as needed
Salt	as needed
Palm oil	1/4 pt.
Dried fish	2 medium
Cray fish -- ground	1 oz.

Whole spinach leaves or young cocoyam leaves

METHOD:

(1)Peel and grate cassava with a grater.

(2)Cut the young cocoyam leaves in sizes of about 3" x 4" or use whole spinach leaf for wrapping.

(3)Rub oil on the bottom of the pot and spread the properly washed cut-off-tail periwinkles on it.

(4)With leaf on left fingers, scoop approximately one half teaspoonful of the grated cassava and roll up using both thumb and fingers. Arrange the rolled-up grated cassava in an orderly fashion inside the pot. Continue until the grated cassava is all wrapped up with leaves. Put in a little water to enable the wrapped grated cassava to harden in steam. Boil for approximately 20 minutes before stirring with a wooden spoon.

(5)Put the ground crayfish, dried fish, salt, accent, etc.

(6)Put in more water and stir gently. Cook for additional 15 minutes.

(7)Add palm oil, lower the heat and simmer for 10-minutes. Serve hot or cold.

Note this: Asa Iwa is also prepared using the same method of Ekpang Nkukwo

CHAPTER FIVE
PREPARATION OF SOUPS & STEWS

ALAPA FRESH MEAT STEW

serves 4

RECIPE:

Fresh meat -- chunks	3 lbs.
Palm oil or vegetable oil	1/2 pt.
Bouillon cubes -- magi cubes	5 cubes
Fresh tomato -chopped	large
Onion -- sliced	1 large
Fresh hot red pepper	to taste
Salt	to taste
Tomato paste -- small	1/2 can
Oregano -- optional	as needed

METHOD:

(1) Boil meat with salt until tender.

(2) Heat oil until smoked.

(3) Into the heated oil, first add chopped onion, after a few seconds, add chopped tomatoes and stir. Add a littel water.

(4) Sprinkle the chunky meat with salt and oregano. Cook for approximately 10 minutes. Stir.

(5) Add bouillon cubes, salt and pepper to taste. Allow to simmer for 5 minutes.

This is best served with, boiled rice, boiled plantains or boiled potatoes.

CHICKEN STEW

Serves 4

RECIPE:

Chicken or hen -- cut	3 lbs.
Palm oil or vegetable oil	1/4 pt.
Onion -- chopped, sliced	2 large
Tomatoes -- fresh chopped	2 medium
Tomato paste	1/2 can
Salt and pepper	to taste
Oregano or curry powder	optional
Magi cubes	4 cubes

METHOD:

(1)Cut chicken or hen into little chunks and boil with salt and chopped onion until tender.

(2)Heat palm oil or vegetable oil in a pot until changes to orange color.

(3)Add first the chopped onion, then fresh chopped tomatoes and stir. Add about 5 spoonful of water.

(4)After 5-minutes, add the boiled chicken or hen and stir. Add approximately 10 tablespoonfuls of water before adding the tomato paste, pepper, salt and boullion cubes. Allow to cook for 10 minutes.

(5)Reduce heat and simmer for 5-minutes. Serve with boiled rice, boiled plantains, boiled yams or boiled potatoes.

MUSHROOM STEW

Serve 3

RECIPE

Mushroom [sliced]	3lbs
Vegetable oil	1/2 lb
Onion [sliced]	1 onion
Fresh tomato [sliced]	1 medium size
Salt and pepper	to taste

METHOD

1. Heat the vegetable oil in a pot until smokes.

2. Fry the onion,then the chopped tomatoes.

3. Put the chopped mushrooms and fry.

Then the mushroom stew is now ready and can be served with boiled rice or yam.

FRESH FISH STEW

serves 4

RECIPE:

Fresh fish -- cut	3 lbs.
Fresh tomatoes	2 medium
Palm oil or vegetable oil	1/2 pt.
Bouillon cubes	4 cubes
Onion -- sliced, ground	2 medium
Hot red pepper and salt	to taste
Tomato paste	1 tin
Water -- approximately	1/2cup

METHOD:

(1)Heat vegetable oil in a pot until smokes. Add sliced onions first, then sliced fresh tomatoes.

(2)After five minutes, add the already dressed cut fresh fish. Stir gently with a wooden spoon.

(3)Add approximately 10 tablespoonfuls of water before adding tomato paste, bouillon cubes, salt and pepper as needed.

(4)Allow to simmer for 5-minutes. Add a little water as needed.

Serve with boiled rice, dodo or boiled potatoes.

FRESH SHRIMP STEW

serves 5

RECIPE:

Fresh shrimps	2 lbs.
Palm oil or vegetable oil	1/2 pint
Bouillon cubes -- magi cubes	4 cubes
Fresh tomatoes	2 medium
Onion	1 large
Fresh hot red pepper	to taste
Salt	to taste
Tomato paste -- small	1/2 can

METHOD:

(1)Dress shrimps by removing shells. Prepare all <u>recipe</u> as with fresh fish stew .

(2)Heat palm oil until smoked.

(3)First add chopped onion, then chopped fresh tomatoes.

(4)Sprinkle shrimps with salt before putting into the pot after approximately 2 minutes. Put about 10 tablespoonfuls of water. Add tomato paste and stir gently. Cook for 10 minutes.

(5)Add boullion cubes, salt and pepper as needed.

(6)Allow to simmer for 5 minutes.

This is best served with boiled rice, boiled yams, boiled potatoes or boiled plantains.

SPINACH SOUP STEW

serves 4

RECIPE:

Spinach	2 lbs.
Salt and hot red pepper	as needed

METHOD:

(1)Chop the spinach.

(2)Boil with 1 pt. of water, salt and pepper for approximately 10 minutes.

To make a bowl of spinach soup stew, mix this boiled spinach with the already prepared shrimp stew or fresh fish stew in the ratio of 2:1, that is two parts of the boiled spinach to one part of the above cooked stew. This could be used to eat any foo foo.

OKRA SOUP STEW

serves 3

RECIPE:

Okra-- ground	1 lb
Salt and pepper	to taste
Potash --	optional

METHOD:

Boil ground okra in 1 pt. of water. Add salt, and red pepper.

Boil for 10 minutes.

To make a bowl of okra soup stew, mix the cooked okra with the already prepared fresh fish or chicken stew in the ratio of 2:1 ie. two parts of the cooked okra to one part of the stew.

Serve with pounded yam, amala, ekpang or any foo foo

GBEGIRI

(bean stew)

serves 6

RECIPE

Black eyed peas	3 lbs
Fresh tomatoes -- chopped	2 large

Dried fish -- chopped	2 large
Okra -- cut	1 lb
Potash -- ground	1 teaspoonful
Onion -- chopped	1 large
Salt and pepper	as needed
Okra -- chopped	1 lb
Spinach -- chopped	1 lb

METHOD

1. Boil beans until soft. Add dried fish, onions, tomatoes, salt, pepper as needed, okra and spinach. Cook for 15 minutes. Stir continuously to avoid burning. Add more water if necessary.

Serve with any foo foo.

RICE AND BEAN PORRIDGE

Serves 5

RECIPE:

Rice	2 lbs.
Beans -- black eye peas	1 lb.
Palm oil or vegetable oil	1/4 pt.
Cray fish -- ground	1/2 oz.
Salt and pepper	to taste
Meat -- chopped	2 lbs
Dried fish -- cut into pieces	1 large
Tomatoes -- fresh	3 medium

Tomato paste--small	1/2 can
Boullion cubes or accent	as needed
Onion -- chopped	1 large
Shrimps -- optional	1 lb.

METHOD:

(1)Boil beans in a pot until soft.

(2)Add more water and rice, and continue boiling.

(3)In a separate pot, boil meat until tender.

(4)In the bean and rice pot, add crayfish, meat, dried fish, fresh tomato, tomato paste, onion, shrimps, boullion cubes or accent, salt and pepper as needed. Cook until rice softens.

(6)Add palm or vegetable oil. Allow to simmer for 5 minutes.

Serve hot or cold as a meal.

EWA

(bean porridge)

serves 4

RECIPE:

Black eyed peas (beans]	3 lbs.
Large bell pepper - chopped	1 large
Dried fish -- chopped	2 medium
Salt and pepper	to taste
Onion -- chopped	one large

Tomatoes - fruit- chopped	2 medium
Tomato paste -- small	1/2 can

METHOD:

(1) First boil the black eyed pea beans until soft.

(2) Cut the dried fish into desirable pieces and add.

(3) Add onion, tomatoes, pepper and salt as needed.

(4) After cooking and simmering for 10 minutes, turn off the heat.

Ewa is eaten with stew and it can be served with boiled yam, boiled plantains or boiled rice.

PREPARATION OF DIFFERENT KINDS OF SOUPS

African soups are prepared for different purposes such as for eating foo foo. Another type of soup is prepared with meat such as goat meat, beef, chicken, fresh fish etc. and is used for drinking palm juice, beer,coca cola, fresh milk or any beverage. The usual name for it is pepper soup (ngwo ngwo).

PEANUT SOUP

serves 4

RECIPE:

Onion -- chopped	1 large
Roasted peanuts or peanut butter	1 lb.
Meat	3 lbs.
Fresh tomatoes -- chopped	2 large

Salt and pepper   to taste

Water 1/4 gal or as needed

Spinach 2lbs

METHOD:

(1)Smoothly grind roasted peanuts or use peanut butter.

(2)Cut meat into little chunks and boil.

(3)Blend the ground peanuts or peanut butter to form a watery paste.

(4)Add fresh chopped tomatoes, onions, meat, spinach,salt and pepper as needed in a pot of approximately 1 quart of water. Cook for 10 minutes.

(5)Allow the soup to simmer in a low heat for 5-minutes.

Serve with pounded yam, tuwo chinkafa or eba.

EGUSI SOUP

(mellon ball soup)

serves 4

RECIPE:

Mellon seeds (egusi) -- ground	10 oz.
Palm oil or vegetable oil	1/4 pt
Spinach or water leaf -- chopped	1 lb
Onions - ground	2 medium
Salt and pepper	as needed
Maggi cubes	3 cubes
Fresh tomatoes	2 medium

Cray fish -- ground	1 oz
Dried fish -- cut	2 medium

RECIPE

(1) Grind mellon seeds, pepper, crayfish, onions and fresh tomatoes.

(2) Mix all ingredients together with a little water to form a mild dough. Divide this mixture into two portions.

(3) Add one portion of the ground melons to a pot containing approximately one quart of water, crayfish, onion and fresh tomatoes. Allow content to boil.

(4) Make the other portion of the ground melon, into small balls of approximately 1/2 inch in diameter. Add the melon balls into the pot. Stir gently, then add chopped spinach, maggi and oil. Cook for 10 minutes. Simmer for 5 minutes.

Best served with ekpang, tuwo chinkafa or boiled yam.

NOTE: Plain egusi is cooked with spinach without the egusi balls.

NOTE THAT THERE IS A PROCESSED DRIED AND FRESH BITTER LEAF AVAILABLE IN YOUR NEAREST AFRICAN FOOD STORES. LOOK IN YELLOW PAGES UNDER GROCERS. THE WEIGHT FOR THE DRIED BITTER LEAF IS USUALLY ONE OUNCE PER BAG, AND THAT OF THE FRESH BITTER LEAF IS ONE POUND PER

BAG. GOING THROUGH THE PROCESS OF REMOVING THE BITTERNESS IS UNNECESSARY. THIS IS ONLY DONE WHEN THE PROCESSED BITTER LEAF IS NOT AVAILABLE.

BITTER LEAF EGUSI SOUP

serves 6

RECIPE

Melon seeds (egusi)	5 oz
Bitter leaf -- fresh	1 lb
Palm oil	1/2 pt.
Spinach -- chopped	1 lb
Onion -- chopped	1 medium
Salt and pepper	as needed
Maggi cubes	3 cubes
Cray fish -- ground	1 oz
Dried fish	2 medium

METHOD

1. Grind melon seeds, pepper, crayfish and onion.

2. Put all ingredients in a pot containing approximately one pint of water and cook.

3. Then, add ground melon, spinach, and bitter leaf. Cook for 15 minutes. Stir.

4. Add oil and allow to simmer for 5 minutes.

Serve with any foo foo.

EGUSI AGBONO SOUP

<u>RECIPE</u>

Egusi -- ground	3 oz
Agbono seeds -- ground	3 oz
Meat -- chopped	2 lbs
Onion	1 large
Bitter leave	3 oz
Spinach	2lbs
Palm oil	1/4 pint
Fresh tomatoes	2 large
Dried fish	1 large
Cray fish	1 oz

Salt and pepper as needed

<u>METHOD</u>

1. Put oil in a pot and heat lightly. Add agbono and fry. Then add approximately I pint of water, meat, onion, tomatoes, dried fish, cray fish, egusi, bitter leaf and spinach. Add salt and pepper as needed. Cook for 15 minutes. Simmer for 5 minutes.

Serve with any foo foo.

BITTER LEAF AGBONO SOUP

RECIPE:

Agbono -- (bush mango seeds)	4 oz.
Palm oil (vegetable oil)	1/4 pt.
Dried cray fish - ground	1 oz.
Salt and pepper -- ground	to taste
Dried fish -- chunks	2 lbs.
Bitterleaf -- fresh	1 lb.
Maggi or boullion -- optional	4 cubes.
Stock fish	8 pieces

METHOD:

(1) Grind Agbono, crayfish and pepper.

(2) Scrub the bitterleaf in order to remove some of the bitterness or purchase the processed one in the African food store.

(3) Add dried fish, crayfish, stock fish ,salt and pepper in a pot of approximately 1 quart of water and allow to cook for 5 minutes.

(4) First mix agbono with a small quantity of oil before putting into the pot. The lumpy formation made by the agbono should be cleared by smashing with a spoon.

(5) Add bitterleaf and palm oil. Cook for 10 minutes. Allow to simmer for 5 minutes.

Serve with ekpang, foo foo or eba.

SPINACH AGBONO SOUP

serves 4

RECIPE:

Agbono -- ground	1 lb.
Palm oil or vegetable oil	1/4 pt.
Onion -- chopped	1 large
Meat -- chopped	2 lbs.
Dried fish -- chopped	2 lbs
Cray fish -- ground	1 oz
Salt and pepper -- ground	as needed
Spinach --chopped	1 lb.

METHOD:

(1)Grind agbono, cray fish and pepper.

(2)Squeeze the bitterleaf in order to remove some of its bitterness or use the processed bitter leaf.

(3)In a pot of approximately 1 quart of water, add dry fish, crayfish, salt and pepper. Cook for 5 minutes.

(4)First, mix ground agbono with a small quantity of oil before putting into the pot. Cook for 10 minutes. Lumps formation made by agbono can be cleared up by beating with a spoon in a plate. Add spinach and palm oil. Allow to simmer for 5 minutes.

Serve with ekpang or foo-foo.

BITTER LEAF OKRA SOUP

serves 5

RECIPE:

Bitterleaf - dried processed	1 oz
Okra -- cut	1 lb
Onions -- cut	2 medium
Palm oil or vegetable oil	1/4 pt.
Fresh tomatoes -- chopped	2 medium
Salt and pepper	as needed
Meat -- chopped	3 lbs
Cray fish -- ground	1 oz

METHOD:

1) Squeeze the bitterleaf to remove most of its bitterness or purchase a fresh processed bitter leaf from the African food store.

2) Cut okra and onions into tiny pieces.

3) In a pot of approximately 1-1/4 pts. of water, add the chopped meat, bitter leaf, onions, okra, pepper, salt, crayfish and palm oil. Cook for approximately 10 minutes. Simmer for 5-minutes.

Serve well with any foo-foo.

EFO SOUP

(green leafy vegetable soup)

serves 5

RECIPE:

Any green vegetable - chopped	3 lbs
Onion -- chopped	1 medium
Red pepper	as needed
Palm oil or vegetable oil	1/2 pint
Salt	as needed
Dried fish or stock fish	2 lbs
Meat -- goat	2 lbs
Fruit tomatoes -- chopped	2 medium
Cray fish -- ground	1 oz

METHOD:

1) Cut meat into pieces and boil to desirable tenderness.

2) Wash dried fish and cut into suitable pieces.

3) Cut stock fish into pieces as preferred.

4) Put the fish, stock fish, and meat into a pot and fry in oil with all the ground ingredients.Then add about 2 cups of water. After 5 minutes, add the chopped vegetable and ground dried crayfish. Allow to simmer for 15-minutes.

Serve with eba or amala.

Note: The leafy vegetable can be spinach, fluted pumpkin, green or waterleaf.

EWEDU SOUP

(slimy vegetable soup)

serves 6

RECIPE:

Ewedu leaf -- chopped	2 lbs
Salt	to taste
Potash -- optional	just enough
Red pepper	as needed
Cray fish	2 oz
Fermented African locust beans -- optional	
Fish -- chopped	2 medium
Meat -- chopped	2 lbs

METHOD:

1) Chop ewedu leaf, and place in the pot.

2) Bring to boil in a pot containing 1-1/2 pints of water and Ewedu.

3) Constantly stir with a wire-like kind of spoon as to make it draw and more slimy.

4) Add ground crayfish, pepper, salt, fish, meat and potash.

5) Watch to avoid boil over. Keep the pot open.

6) Allow to simmer for 5-minutes.

Ewedu is served with amala or any other kind of foo foo.

BITTER LEAF SOUP

serves 4

RECIPE:

Bitter leaf -- fresh	1 lb
Spinach -- chopped	1 lb
Onion -- cut	1 medium
Palm oil	1/4 pint
Salt and pepper	as needed
Cray fish -- ground	1 oz
Dried fish cut in pieces	2 medium
Meat -- boiled and chopped	2 lbs

METHOD:

1) Purchase one pound of fresh processed or dried processed bitter leaf in African food store.

2) Into a pot, put onion, pepper, salt, crayfish, meat and fish together. Book with 1 pint of water.

3) Add spinach and bitter leaf together. Cook for 15 minutes.

4) Add palm oil and allow to simmer for 5 minutes.

Serve with any kind of foo-foo.

PREPARATION OF CONGO MEAT

(Snails)

Snails are properly dressed using the following steps:

(a) Remove snail from its shell by forcing it out.

(b)Sprinkle it with enough quantity of salt and knead with hands until most of the slime is removed.

(c)Squeeze and sprinkle with lime juice until all the slime is removed.

(d)Wash off with clean water. The snail is now dressed and is ready to be used with the following recipe.

RECIPE:

Snails	10 snails
Salt and pepper	as needed
Vegetable oil	1/2 pint
Onion and tomatoes	as needed

METHOD:

1)Slice the dressed snails in halves.

2)Heat the vegetable oil.

3)Cut onion and tomatoes into little pieces.

4)Fry onion first, then the chopped tomatoes.

5)Add the sliced dressed snails and fry for about 10 minutes.

Serve with any beverage or milk.

CONGO MEAT BITTER LEAF SOUP

serves 4

RECIPE:

Bitter leaf -- fresh	1 lb.
Spinach -- chopped	1 lb.

Onion -- chopped	one large
Palm oil	1/4 pt.
Salt and pepper	as needed
Crayfish -- ground	1 oz.
Congo meat -- snails	10 pieces

METHOD:

1. Use fresh processed bitter leaf.
2. Dress snails as explained in the preparation of congo meat.
3. In a pot containing approximately 1 1/2 quarts of water put onions, crayfish, snails, salt and pepper as needed. Allow to boil for 2 minutes.
4. Then add the bitter leaf, spinach and oil. Cook and simmer for 15-minutes.

Serve with amala, ekpang, farina or semolina foo foo.

AFIA EFERE EBOT

(white goat meat soup)

serves 4

RECIPE:

Goat meat -- cut	2 lbs
Mashed potatoes	2 tablespoonfuls
Salt and pepper	as needed
Wing bean (uyayak) --	roasted to form charcoal
Oregano	as needed

Onion - chopped	1 large
Dried fish -- chopped	1 medium
Cray fish -- ground	1 oz

METHOD:

1. Cut goat meat into pieces and boil until soft.

2. Into the pot of approximately one pint of water, put salt, pepper, cray fish, oregano and ground roasted uyayak, dried fish and goat meat. Cook for 5 minutes.

3. Add mashed potatoes as needed to produce a little watery paste soup. Cook for 10 minutes.

4. Simmer for 5 minutes.

Serve with pounded yam, or eba.

EDIKANG IKONG SOUP

(fried spinach soup)

serves 5

RECIPE:

Cray fish -- ground	1 oz.
Red pepper and salt	as needed
Periwinkles	[optional] 1 lb.
Onion -- chopped	1 large
Meat – goat or beef meat	2 lbs.
Palm oil	1 pt.
Dried fish -- cut	1 lb.
Spinach (or vegetable pumpkin)	2 lb.

Stock fish	1 lb.
Magi cubes or accent	4 cubes

METHOD:

1. Heat the palm oil until hot and do not allow it to smoke.

2. Add a little water to prevent scourging ,add the already prepared ingredients ,like fish ,cray fish, meat, onion, tomatoes, stock fish ,periwinkle, salt and pepper, accent or magi cube .

    Add the prepared spinach and allowed to cook for 15 minutes.

3. Stir occasionally to ensure that the ingredients mix properly. Be careful not to put too much water because this soup need more oil than water. Simmer for 5 mins

Serve with foo foo, boiled yam, amala ,pounded yam or boiled rice.

NWUP SOUP

(mixed vegetable soup)

serves 5

RECIPE

Spinach -- chopped	1/2 lb
Fluted pumpkin leaf -- chopped	1/2 lb
Green vegetable -- chopped	1/2 lb
Palm oil	1/2 pt.
Cray fish -- chopped	1 oz

Dried fish -- chunks	2 medium
Stock fish -- chunks	6 pieces
Salt and pepper	as needed
Maggi cubes	4 cubes

METHOD

1. Into a pot of boiling water, put in the following ingredients; ground crayfish, magi cubes, dried fish, stock fish,salt and pepper as needed. Boil for 5 minutes.

2. Add spinach, fluted pumpkin and green vegetables. Cook for 10 minutes. Add oil. Allow to simmer for 5 minutes then, turn off the heat.

Serve with foo foo, boiled plantain or boiled yam.

UKPOTORO SOUP

(Ibaba)

serves 5

RECIPE

Ukpotoro (ibaba) ground peeled	12 seeds
Meat -- chunks	2 lbs
Salt and pepper	as needed
Cray fish	1 oz
Onions	2 medium
Dried fish	1 medium
Spinach -- chopped	2 lbs

METHOD

1. Peel off ibaba seeds and boil for over 45 minutes.

2. Grate the ibaba in a grater or ground in a blender.

3. Put approximately one pint of water in a pot and boil.

Put in all ingredients -- meat, crayfish, onion, salt and pepper and dried fish.

4. Blend the grated ibaba with water before putting into the boiling pot. Add spinach and cook for 15 minutes. Then simmer in a low heat for 5 minutes.

Serve with any foo foo.

OWO SOUP

(potash soup)

serves 4

RECIPE:

Dried bush meat or wild game-- cut	3 lbs.
Dried fish -- chopped	1 lb.
Ground potash	1/4 oz.
Palm oil or vegetable oil	1/4 pt.
Cray fish -- ground	1 oz.
Salt and pepper	as needed
Fresh tomatoes -- chopped	2 medium
Onion - chopped	1 large
Water	1 pint

METHOD:

1. Cut meat into desirable pieces and boil properly in a pot.

2.Combine fish, crayfish, fresh tomatoes, onion, salt and pepper in a pot and put little water as needed.

3.After cooking for 5-minutes, turn off the heat to cool.

4.Add palm oil and ground potash and stir. No more application of heat. The orange creamy appearance of the sauce is an indication that owo soup is now ready.

Serve with boiled rice, yams or boiled plantains.

OKRA SOUP

(efere etighi)

serves 4

RECIPE:

Okra -- ground & chopped	1 lb.
Onion -- chopped	1 large
Palm oil -- vegetable oil	1/4 pt.
Salt and pepper	as needed
Fresh tomatoes -- chopped	2 large
Meat or dried fish - - chopped	2 lbs
Cray fish -- ground	1 oz
Water -- approximately	2 pts.

METHOD:

1.Split okra into two parts. Grind one part and chop the other.

2.In a pot of water combine pepper, onion, fish, crayfish, meat, tomatoes, ground okra, salt and pepper as needed. Cook for 5 minutes.

3.Add oil and the chopped okra and allow to continue cooking for 5 minutes, then simmer with a low heat for another 5 minutes.

4.Note: The okra should not be fully cooked.

Serve best with ekpang and any foo-foo.

VEGETABLE OKRA SOUP

serves 5

RECIPE

Okra -- chopped and ground	1 lb
Spinach -- chopped	1 lb
Onion -- chopped	1 large
Salt and pepper -	as needed
Palm oil	1/4 pint
Fresh tomatoes	2 medium
Meat -- chunks	2 lbs
Dried fish -- chunks	1 lb
Cray fish -- ground	1 oz

METHOD

1. Split okra into two parts. Grind one part and chop the other.

2. In a pot of water combine pepper, onion, dried fish, crayfish, tomatoes, ground okra, salt and pepper as needed. Cook for 5 minutes.

3. Add chopped spinach and chopped okra and allow to cook for 5 minutes. Then add palm oil. Simmer for 5 minutes.

NOTE: The okra and the vegetable should not be fully cooked.

Serve with any foo foo.

ILA SOUP

(okra soup)

serves 5

RECIPE:

Okra --- ground	1 lb.
Meat --- chunks	2 lbs.
Vegetable oil	1/4 pt.
Cray fish --- ground	1 oz
Locust beans (iru) -- optional	2 oz.

METHOD:

(1)Grate okra in a blender.

(2)Cook meat until tender.

(3)Add approximately 1 pint of water to the meat in a pot and boil.

(4)Add crayfish, locust beans to give flavor, salt and pepper as needed. Cook for 10 minutes.

(5)Add the ground okra,then oil. Simmer for 5-mins.

This is served with eba, amala or ekpang.

FRESH FISH OKRA SOUP

(white soup)

serves 5

RECIPE:

Fresh cat fish	3 large
Okra -- chopped	1 lb
Salt and pepper	as needed
Oregano	as needed
Onion -- chopped	1 large
Tomatoes -- optional	1 large

METHOD:

(1)Cut cat fish or any other fresh fish into required sizes and boil with very little water.

(2)Put in all the ingredients including salt and pepper as needed. Put approximately one pint of water.

(3)Allow to cook for 15-minutes.

Fresh fish okra soup is now ready to be served with any foo-foo.

GUMBO SOUPS

The name "Gumbo" is African name for okra. It was imported to the United States by African slaves and it is now becoming one of the most important dishes of New Orleans, Lousiana.

CRAB MEAT AND SHRIMP GUMBO

serves 4

RECIPE

Okra - big chunks	1 lb
Shrimps	1 lb
Crab meat	1 lb
Red pepper, salt, curry or nutmeg --	as needed
Onion -- chopped	3 large onions
Tomato paste -- small	1 can
Fresh tomatoes -- chopped	3 large
Cray fish -- ground	1/2 oz
Celery -- Chopped	4 stalks

METHOD

1. Cut okra into big chunks.
2 Put 1 quart of water in a pot and boil. Add crayfish, tomato paste, cut onion, celery, salt, crab meat, shelled shrimps, okra, nutmeg or curry powder as needed. Allow content to remain cooking for 10 mins. Then, simmer at a reduced heat for 5 minutes.

Turn off heat and serve hot with boiled rice or boiled potatoes.

FRESH FISH GUMBO

serves 5

<u>RECIPE</u>

Okra -- cut in big chunks	2 lbs
Fresh fish -- cut and boiled	3 medium
Celery -- chopped	10 oz
Pepper, salt, curry -	as needed.
Tomato paste -- small	1 can
Onions	2 large
Magi cubes or bullions cubes	3 cubes
Fresh tomatoes -- chopped	3 medium
Cray fish	1/2 oz

<u>METHOD</u>

1. Cut okra in big chunks.
2. Put approximately 1 quart of water in a pot and boil with the following ingredients; crayfish, tomato paste, onions, maggi cubes and celery.
3. Add salt, pepper, nutmeg or curry powder as needed.
4. Add the boiled fresh fish and okra. Allow to cook for 10 minutes.

Serve with boiled yam, boiled potatoes or boiled rice.

CHICKEN GUMBO

serves 4

<u>RECIPE</u>

Okra -- big chunks	I lb
Hen (whole hen)--chopped	2 lbs
Celery -- cut	10 oz
Pepper, salt and curry -	as neeeded
Tomato paste	1 small can
Fresh tomatoes -- chopped	2 large
Onions -- chopped	2 medium
Maggi or boullion cubes	4 cubes
Cray fish	1/2 oz

<u>METHOD</u>

1. Cook whole hen in a pot until tender.

2. Carefully remove all bones while cutting the hen into pieces.

3. Put approximately 1 quart of water in a pot and boil with onions, celery, fresh tomatoes, crayfish, tomato paste, maggi cubes. Add salt, pepper, and curry powder as needed. Cook for 5 minutes.

4. Add okra and the boneless pieces of hen. Cook for another 5 minutes then, simmer for 5 minutes in a low heat.

Serve with boiled rice, boiled potatoes or boiled yams.

BITTER-LEAF SHRIMP GUMBO SOUP

serves 5

RECIPE:

Bitter leaf -- fresh processed	1 lb.
Okra -- chunks	1 lb.
Onion -- chopped	1 large
Fresh tomatoes -- chopped	3 small
Shrimps -- shelled	2 lbs
Magi or bouillon cubes - to taste or	3 cubes
Salt and pepper	as needed

METHOD:

(1)Chop onion, okra, tomatoes into little pieces. Remove shells from the shrimps.

(2)Put the ingredients in a pot except bitter leaf. Bring to boil.

(3)After boiling, add the bitter leaf and oil and let it simmer for 10 minutes in a low heat.

Serve with boiled plantains, boiled yams, or boiled rice.

OTONG SOUP

(slimy okra soup)

serves 5

RECIPE:

Spinach or fluted pumpkin leaf	1 lb.
Okra -- chopped	1 lb.

Cray fish -- ground	1 oz.
Potash (akanwu) --approx.	1/4 diameter
Red pepper and salt	as needed
Dried fish -- chopped	2 medium
Palm oil or vegetable oil	1/2 pt.
Shelled dressed periwinkles	2 lbs. (optional)

METHOD:

(1) Chop spinach or African fluted pumpkin leaves into pieces.

(2) Split okra into two halves. Grind one half and chop the other.

(3) Grind crayfish and pepper. Cut the dried fish into small desired sizes.

(4) Put the fish, pepper, salt, periwinkles into the boiling pot and boil for 5-minutes.

(5) Add both the chopped and ground okra, vegetable and then, potash. Cook for 10 mins. Then add oil and let it simmer for 5 minutes. Stir constantly.

NOTE: Otong soup is cooked without lid. Stir continuously to avoid boiled over.

Best served with ekpang or eba.

BANGA SOUP WITH UKAZI

(ukazi palm fruit cream soup)

serves 5

Note: Review how banga (palm fruit cream) was prepared with palm fruits. Also, the processed palm fruit cream is available in African food stores.

RECIPE

Afang (ukazi) -- ground	1 oz.
Palm fruit cream --	2 cans or 1/4 gallon
Dried fish -- pieces	2 large
Cray fish -- ground	1 oz.
Periwinkles -- optional	1 lb.
Salt and red pepper	as needed
Maggi cubes or accent to taste	4 cubes

METHOD:

(1)Dress periwinkles by cutting off tails. Wash thoroughly in water.

(2)Put the washed periwinkles in a pot containing approximately 2 quarts of palm fruit cream. If canned palm fruit cream is used then, add approximately 1 pint of water.

(3)Then, add all these ingredients and cook for 15- minutes.

Best served with ekpang, amala or eba.

NOTE: The leafy vegetable for cooking the cream soup can be spinach, fluted pumpkin, green or water-leaf.

OTONG SOUP WITH AFRICAN OIL BEAN SEEDS AND RED BEANS

(special soup eaten by Oron people)

serves 5

RECIPE

Red beans -- boil	1 lb
Fermented oil bean seeds	1 lb
Okra -- ground	1/2 lb
Cray fish -- ground	1 oz
Potash -- ground	1/2 tablespoons
Salt and pepper	as needed
Dried fish	2 medium
Palm oil	1/2 pint
Ewedu leaf (etiyung) or spinach	1/2 lb

METHOD

1. Boil the red beans for 80 minutes or until soft.

2. Into a boiling pot, put approximately one quart of water. Put in the soft boiled red beans, cray fish, fermented oil beans, dried fish , salt and pepper as needed. Cook for 15 minutes then add leaf, okra, potash and palm oil. Add the potash .Do not cover the pot. Stir constantly to avoid boiled over. Simmer for 5 minutes.

Serve with ekpang or any foo foo.

BANGA GOAT MEAT WITH ATAMA SOUP

(palm fruit cream soup with atama and goat meat)

serves 5

RECIPE:

Goat meat -- cut	2 lbs.
Palm fruit cream -	1 can or palm fruit cream
Dried fish	1 large.
Cray fish	1 oz.
Shelled periwinkles	2 lbs. (optional)
Salt and pepper	as needed.
Maggi cubes 4 or accent	as needed.
Atama leaf -- ground	1 oz.

METHOD:

(1) Dress periwinkles by cutting off tails and washing properly.

(2) Put them into a pot containing 1 quart of palm fruit cream. Boil.

(3) Put all ingredients and cook for 15 minutes.

Serve with ekpang or amala.

PLAIN BANGA SOUP WITH ATAMA

(Palm fruit cream soup using atama leaf)

serves 5

RECIPE:

Beef-- chopped	3 lbs.
Dried atama leaf -- ground	2 oz.
Palm fruit cream --	2 cans or 1 quart.
Dried fish --- chopped	1 large.
Cray fish - ground	1 oz.
Salt and red pepper	as needeed.
Maggi cubes 4 or accent	as needed.

METHOD:

Just cook like the above method .

In a pot containing one quart of palm fruit cream, add all the above ingredients and cook for 15 minutes.

Best served with ekpang or eba.

NGWO NGWO

(pepper soup)

serves 4

This particular soup is best prepared with different parts of animal usually goat or bush meat such as the intestines, lungs, liver, legs, tripes or the stomach, etc. Meat can be used too. All parts are thoroughly washed and cut into pieces and cook together. It is generally used for drinking ,beer, fresh milk or any beverage.

<u>RECIPE</u>:

Goat's parts: tripes, liver, intestines	3 lbs.
Salt and pepper	as needed
Onion -- chopped	1 large
Fresh tomatoes	2 large
Crayfish --optional	1 oz.
Boullion cubes or accent	as needed
Oregano	as needed

<u>METHOD</u>:

(1) Dress various parts of goat by cleaning and thoroughly washing with water. Put the parts into a pot with approximately one quart of water. Cook meat to your desirable tenderness.

(2) Add salt and boil until tender. Put about 1 pint of water.

(3) Add crayfish, pepper, oregano, accent, onions and salt as needed. Cook for 15-mins.

Serve with cold drink or fresh milk.

BUSH MEAT PEPPER SOUP.

serves 3

<u>RECIPE</u>:

Bush meat -- chopped	3 lbs.

Salt and pepper	to taste.
Maggi cubes	3 cubes.
Cray fish -- ground	1 oz.
Bell pepper	1 large.
Oregano	as needed

METHOD:

(1)Chop bush meat and boil until tender.

(2)Into a pot containing approximately 1 qt. of water, add all ingredients and cook for 10-minutes.

Serve with palm juice or cold soft drink or beer.

CHICKEN PEPPER SOUP

serves 4

RECIPE:

Hen -- chopped	3 lbs.
Salt and hot red pepper	as needed
Cray fish -- ground	1 oz.
Large bell pepper -- chopped	1 pepper
Boullion or accent	to taste
Oregano	as needed
Onion -- chopped	1 large

METHOD:

1.Chop and boil hen until tender.

2.Put all ingredients in a pot of 1 pint of water and bring the content to boil.

3.Reduce heat and allow to simmer for 5-minutes.

Serve with fresh milk or any beverage.

FRESH FISH PEPPER SOUP

serves 5

RECIPE:

Fresh fish -- cat fish	4 large
Salt and red pepper	as needed
Crayfish -- ground -- optional	1 oz.
Mashed potatoes -- optional	2 tablespoonfuls
Large bell pepper -- chopped	1 large
Tomatoes -- chopped	2 tomatoes
Accent or bouillon cubes.	2 cubes
Onion -- chopped	1 large
Oregano	as needed

METHOD:

1.Sprinkle the dressed and chopped cat fish with salt. Boil with approximately 10-spoonfuls of water for 5-minutes.

2.Add about 1.5 pints of water.

3.Add onion, pepper, salt, tomato, oregano, bell pepper and bouillon cubes. Cook for 10 minutes.

4.Then, add a little mashed potatoes just to give a little watery paste soup and allow to simmer for 5-minutes.

Serve with milk or any beverage ,tea or coffee

GOAT MEAT PEPPER SOUP

serves 5

RECIPE:

Goat meat -- chopped	4 lbs.
Cray fish -- ground	1/2 oz.
Salt and pepper	as needed
Mashed potatoes -- optional	2 tablespoons
Bell pepper	1 large
Oregano	as needed
Accent or bouillon cubes	4 cubes

METHOD:

(1) Boil goat meat until tender. Put approximately 1.5 pints of water in a pot and boil with the following ingredients; cray fish, oregano, pepper, salt and bouillon cubes. Cook for 10 mins.

(2) Then add two tablespoonfuls of mashed potatoes and allow to simmer for 5 minutes.

This is served with fresh milk or any beverage, tea or coffee.

BEEF OR GOAT MEAT PEPPER SOUP WITH POTATOES AND PLANTAIN

RECIPE

Beef or goat meat	2lbs
Potatoes [chunks]	3lbs

Green plantain [cut in chunks]	4 large
Salt and pepper	to taste
Onion [chopped]	1 onion
Oregano	to taste
Potash	[a pinch]
Crayfish about	I oz
Bouillon cube or accent	5 cubes

METHOD

1. Cook the meat to your desirable tenderness.

2. Cut the plantain into chunks and slice the potatoes in halves. Put all into the pot and put about one or two cups of water and cook.

3. Add the chopped onion, salt, pepper, potash ,crayfish and stir with a wooden spoon. Allow to cook for about 30 minutes as to enable the broth to thicken.

Serve on its own as a complete meal.

STOCK FISH PEPPER SOUP

Serves 4

RECIPE:

Stock fish -- chopped	15 pieces
Crayfish -- ground	1/2 oz.
Salt and pepper	as needed
Mashed potatoes - as needed or	2 tablespoonfuls
Large bell pepper	1 large
Oregano	as needed

Magi cubes   3 cubes

METHOD:

(1) Soak stock fish in water and place in a refrigerator overnight.

(2) Into a pot containing approximately 1 1/2 pts. of water, add all the above ingredients in the specified proportion.

(3) Allow to boil and simmer for 10-mins.

Serve with milk or fruit juice, tea or coffee.

DRIED SHRIMP PEPPER SOUP

serves 4

RECIPE

Dried shrimps	5 oz
Onion	1 large
Oregano	as needed
Salt and pepper	as needed
Mashed potato	2 tablespoonfuls

METHOD

1. Dress dried shrimps properly by cutting off tails and heads.

2. In a pot containing 1 pint of water, add the shrimps, onion, oregano, salt and pepper as needed. Put a little mashed potato to give a little paste a desirable broth. Cook for 15 minutes.

Serve with boiled rice, potatoes, plantains or any beverage.

UKUOHO SOUP

(ukazi)

serves 7

RECIPE

Ukazi (afang) -- ground	2 oz
Spinach or (water leaf) - cut	2 lbs.
Cray fish -- ground	1 oz
Red pepper and salt	as needed
Onion -- chopped	1 large
Meat	2 lbs.
Palm oil	1 pt.
Dried fish --	cut 1 Pint
Stock fish --	10 pieces.

METHOD:

(1) Cut meat and boil with salt until tender. Cook with approximately 1 pint of water. Add fish, stock fish, onions cray fish, salt and pepper as needed. Stir gently with a wooden spoon.

(2) Add ground ukazi, spinach, and palm oil. Allow to cook for 10-minutes. Then, simmer for 5 minutes.

NOTE: Do not let too much water spoil the taste of this soup, so be careful with adding water.

Serve with eba and foo-foo.

CASSAVA LEAF SOUP

serves 6

<u>RECIPE</u>

Cassava leaf -- ground	2 lbs
Spinach -- chopped	1/2 lb
Cray fish -- ground	1 oz
Salt and pepper	as needed
Onions -- chopped	2 large
Meat -- chunks	2 lbs
Palm oil	1 pint.
Dried fish	1 large
Stock fish	10 pieces

<u>METHOD</u>

1. Boil meat with salt until tender.
2. Into the boiling pot, add all ingredients - onions, crayfish, dried fish, stock fish, salt and pepper as needed except cassava leaf, spinach and palm oil. Cook with approximately one pint of water for 5 minutes.
3. Add the cassava leaf and spinach, then palm oil. Cook for 30 minutes. Simmer for 5 minutes in a low heat.

Turn off heat.

Serve with any foo foo.

CHAPTER SIX
AFRICAN SNACKS
AND
DRINKS

FURAR GERO

(rice & millet balls)

serves 4

RECIPE:

Ground Rice	2 lbs.
Millet (gero) -- ground)	2 lbs.
Salt & pepper	as needed
Fresh milk	as needed
Sugar	as needed

METHOD:

1. Mix all ingredients together in a large bowl. Work into a stiff paste.

2. Shape this mixture into small balls of about one inch in diameter and cook in water for approximately 15 minutes.

3. Pour away the water and grind the balls in a blender. Reshape into small balls and roll them on the ground rice flour

   Eat as snack.

This is served with fresh milk or any beverage as breakfast.

MOYIN MOYIN

(Bean pie)

serves 6

RECIPE:

Shrimps -- shelled	2 lb.
Dried fish -- chopped	1 lb.
Red pepper	as needed
Palm oil or vegetable oil	1 pint
Onion -- chopped	1 large
Black eyed pea -- ground	3 lbs.
Boiled eggs -- sliced	3 eggs

METHOD:

1. Soak black-eyed pea beans in water for 60 minutes. You may or may not remove the outer layer.

2. Finely grind the black eyed peas.

3. Add all ingredients together and mix into a thick paste. Add a little water if necessary

4. Pour the mixture into aluminum foil shaped in the form of small bags or just wrap in the foil. Place six clean sticks cut into approximate length of 5 inches in the bottom of the pot to form a layer. Arrange them on the layer in orderly fashion. This is the same way previously did with ekpang.

5. Steam for about 80 minutes or until done.

Serve on its own or with fresh milk or any beverage.

AKARA BEANS

(Bean cake)

serves 4

RECIPE:

Black eyed pea beans -- ground   3 lbs.

Salt and ground pepper -- red   as needed

Onion -- chopped   1 large

Vegetable oil   as needed

METHOD:

1. Soak beans in water for 60 minutes.

2. Finely grind the beans.

3. Put all these ingredients together - salt, pepper, onion and a little quantity of water if necessary. Mix thoroughly in a large bowl to a thick consistency.

4. Heat oil in a deep skillet. Shape the mixture into small balls, of approximately 2 inches in diameter with a spoon or fingers and carefully drop them in the deep oil skillet. Fry in the deep skillet of oil until cooked.

This is served with akamu, milk ,tea or coffee   for breakfast.

AKARA EGUSI

(melon cake)

serves 6

RECIPE:

Melon seeds -- ground	2 lbs.
Onion -- cut	1 large
Salt and pepper	as needed

METHOD:

1. On a stove roast melon seeds in a skillet.

2. Blend in a blender.

3. With little water mix all ingredients into a smooth paste like foo foo dough consistency.

4. Mold the paste into small beautiful balls of about an inch in diameter and carefully drop them in the deep oil skillet.

5. Fry in a deep skillet of oil until brownish.

This can be served with ogi, milk or any beverage.

AKARA RICE

(rice cake)

serves 5

RECIPE

Rice	3 lbs
Sugar	1/2 lb
Banana	6 bananas
Nutmeg	to taste

Oil -- vegetable   as needed

Water   as needed

METHOD

1. Mash banana and mix thoroughly with the ground rice, sugar and nutmeg.

2. Add about 1 pint of water just enough to give the mixture a thick paste.

3. Mold the paste into small balls of approximately 2 inches in diameter in the same manner previously did with the bean cake. Fry about 6 balls at a time in a deep skillet of oil until dark brownish.

This is served with milk or any beverage.

AKARA CASSAVA

(cassava cake)

serves 4

RECIPE

Cassava -- grated   3 lbs

Salt and pepper   as needed

Onion --- chopped   one large

Palm oil (for frying)   1 pt

METHOD

1. Peel cassava, wash and grate.

2. Put the grated cassava in a bag and sqeeze some of its water content.

3. Mix the squeezed grated cassava with a little palm oil, onions, salt and pepper as needed.

4. Mold the mixed grated cassava flat in a form of a circular dimension of approximately 4 inches in diameter and 1/4 inch thick.

5. Heat oil in a pan or skillet. Do not allow the oil to smoke. Use a flat spatula or fork to lift the molded cassava into the frying pan. Fry for approximately 10 minutes at the time. When one side is cooked, carefully turn over the other side and fry until cooked.

The cassava cake is now ready.

Serve with milk or any beverage for lunch or break fast.

EDITA IWA

(Cassava snack)

Serves 4

RECIPE

Cassava	5 lbs
Water	as needed

METHOD

1. Peel cassava and boil for 40 minutes.

2. When cool pour away the water and slice cassava into little pieces .

3. Pour the sliced cassava into a vessel of water and let it sit overnight.

4. Wash and change water and edita iwa is now ready.

This is served with fish or shrimps.

SUYA

(Roasted beef)

Serves 6

RECIPE:

Beef	3 lbs
Ground roasted peanuts	1/4 lb
Onion -- sliced	1 large
Salt and pepper	as needed

METHOD:

1. Slice beef into approximate size of 2 by 8 inches or any sliced length.
2. Sprinkle the sliced beef with salt.
3. Grind peanuts and pepper together.
4. Fasten the sliced beef in a skewer and roast on a charcoal grill.
5. The beef is eaten with the peanut/pepper mixture and sliced raw onions.

Serve with fresh milk or any beverage like tea or coffee.

FRIED CHICKEN

Chicken is fried, just like fried fish or any fried meat.

RECIPE:

Chicken -- cut	2 lbs
Salt/pepper	as needed

METHOD:

1. Cut chicken into little pieces.

2. Sprinkle with salt.

3. Fry in a deep skillet of oil.

Serve with milk or any beverage.

ADUN

(Corn ball porridge)

Serves 5

RECIPE

Corn -- ground	2 lbs
Onion	1 large
Salt and pepper	as needed
Palm oil	1/2 pint

METHOD

1. Grind corn finely in a blender.

2, Heat oil until smokes. Fry onion first then, the ground corn. Stir briskly, the corn will shape itself into small balls.

Serve with any beverage.

NSOKOBI

(Stock fish snack)

serves 5

RECIPE:

Stock fish	12 pieces
Palm oil	1/2 pt.
Salt and pepper	as needed
Potash -- ground	1/2 inch. diameter
Cray fish -- ground	1 oz.

METHOD:

1. Cut stock fish into medium sizes of approximately 2"x 4" and soak overnight in water. If the stock fish is a soft type, soak for only a few hours. Tie with clean strings if necessary to hold it together.

2. In a bowl or mortar, thoroughly mix palm oil, ground potash, crayfish, salt and pepper together with a little water approximately 1/2 pint. This is uncooked sauce as we generally called ----- ground sauce.

3. Apply this sauce to the stock fish and warm up the content on a stove for five minutes. This is what is called nsokobi.

It is served with fresh cold milk or any beverage.

ISI EWU

(goat's head snack)

serves 2

RECIPE:

Goat's head	1 head
Palm oil	1/4 pt.
Salt and pepper	to taste.
Fresh or dried utasi leaf	1/2 oz
Potash -- ground	1/2 diameter
Crayfish -- ground	1/2 oz.
Utasi leaf -- chopped	1/2 oz

METHOD:

1. Properly dress goat's head by burning off its skin in fire. Wash properly in water.

2. In a large pot, boil the goat's head with salt until tender.

3. Chop the head into small pieces.

4. Make an uncooked sauce similar to the one made in the preparation of stock fish snack. Mix the sauce with dried or fresh utasi leaf.

5. Thoroughly mix the chopped goat's head in the sauce.

6. Place the pot on a stove to warm up for 5 minutes. This is isi ewu.

Serve with fresh milk ,beer, tea or coffee

KELEWELE

(chunky fried plantains)

serves 4

<u>RECIPE</u>

Ripe plantains	6 plantains
Onion -- chopped	1 onion
Tomato paste	1/2 can
Salt and pepper	as needed

<u>METHOD</u>

1. Peel and cut plantains into small chunks.
2. Sprinkle the chunky plantains with salt and pepper and mix properly with tomato paste.
3. Fry in a deep skillet of oil until brownish.

Serve hot or cold with any beverage.

AYIBILILI

(boiled corn, black eyed peas and peanuts)

serves 5

<u>RECIPE</u>

Black eyed pea beans	1 lb
Peanuts	1 lb
Corn	1 lb
Coconut	as needed
Salt	as needed

METHOD

1. Soak corn overnight, if fresh, do not soak. Boil until soft.

2. In a separate pot, boil black eyed peas until soft.

3. In another pot, boil peanut until soft.

4. Mix all together -- the boiled corn, peanuts and black eyed peas. Add salt as needed.

Serve with coconut.

OJOJO

(fried grated wateryam)

serves 5

RECIPE

Wateryams cocoyams (grated)	5 lbs
Palm oil or vegetable oil	1 pt
Onions -- chopped	2 onions
Salt and pepper	as needed

METHOD

1. Mix grated wateryams and cocoyams with onions salt and pepper.

2. Mold the mixture into small balls of approximately 2 inches in diameter and fry in a deep skillet of oil until well cooked.

3. Serve with soaked garri or any beverage.

ROASTED MEAT COCKTAIL

serves 4

RECIPE

Meat (goat or beef)	5 lbs
Accent	as needed
Onions -- big chunks	2 large
Mushrooms	as needed
Salt and pepper	as needed

METHOD

1. Cut meat into big chunks. Season with accent salt and pepper.

2. Fasten the meat, mushrooms and onions in alternate fashion in a skewer. Roast on a charcoal grill until brownish.

Serve with any beverage.

ROASTED FISH COCKTAIL

Same as roasted meat cocktail except that fish is used . All methods of preparation are similar.

BANANA AND COCONUT PUDDING

serves 5

RECIPE:

Coconut -- grated	2 coconuts
Bananas -- mash	4 bananas
Eggs	3 eggs
Coconut milk	1/2 pint.
Sugar	1/2 1b.

METHOD:

(1)Thoroughly mix mashed bananas, eggs, coconut and the coconut milk together.

(2)Pour the mixture into a cake or pie dish and bake for 30 minutes at a temperature of 350 degrees.

Serve with any beverage.

OMELETTE

serves 1

RECIPE:

Eggs	3 Large
Bell pepper -- chopped	1 large
Fresh red pepper - chopped	to taste
Onion -- chopped	1/2 medium.
Fresh tomato -- chopped	1/2 medium
Oil (vegetable)	as needed

METHOD:

(1)In a bowl, mix eggs with a spoon or mixer.

(2) Put all ingredients in a bowl and mix together.

(3) Heat a little vegetable oil in a frying pan until hot. Then, pour the mixture of the bowl into the frying pan and fry for 2 minutes. Turn over the other side and fry for 1 minutes or until cooked.

Served with, boiled rice, boiled yam, or boiled plantain and milk.

FRIED FISH IN BATTER

This is example of frying fish in batter which is a thin mixture of flour, milk and eggs .

Make a thin batter mixture and dip the fish to be fried into the mixture and fry.

PREPARATION OF PASTRY

RECIPE

Flour	4 lbs
Oil (vegetable)	1 lb
Margarine or butter	1 lb
Salt	as needed
Water	as needed

METHOD

1. Mix flour with butter or margarine and oil, using fingers or a mixer.

3. Add water by sprinkling over this mixture.

4. Knead until a suitable dough is formed.

5. If it does not knead together or leave the bowl clean it means that the ingredients have not been in a correct proportion. Then, add a little more water or flour until the dough clings and leave the side of the bowl clean.

THE PASTRY IS NOW READY FOR MAKING DIFFERENT KINDS OF PIES.

AFRICAN MEAT PIE

serves 6

RECIPE

Prepare pastry	as stated above
Potatoes -- chunks	1 lb
Corned beef	1 can
Salt and pepper	as needed
Nutmeg or curry powder	as needed

METHOD

1. Place pastry on a table and flatten with a roller.

2. Use a tumbler rim of about 4" in diameter to cut the pastry in circles.

3. Boil potatoes and cut into little chunks.

4. Open corned beef and gently spread over the boiled chunky potatoes and mix gently with a wooden spoon. Sprinkle with pepper, salt, curry powder or nutmeg as needed.

5. Scoop just enough mixture and place on the circular pastry shaped with a tumbler rim.

6. Fold the mixture with the pastry to form a crescent or semi circle. Use fork to seal the semi circle. Continue this with other circular pastry.

7. Place the pie in a pie pan and bake in a pre-heat oven temperature of 350 degrees for 30 minutes.

Serve hot with milk or any beverage.

FISH PIE

serves 4

<u>RECIPE</u>

Prepare pastry as above

Potatoes --- chunks	1 lb
Canned fish --- mash	2 cans
Salt and pepper	to taste
Nutmeg or curry powder	as needed

<u>METHOD</u>

1. Place pastry on a table and flatten with a roller.

2. Use a tumbler rim of approximate size of 4" in diameter to cut the pastry into circles.

3. Boil potatoes and cut into little chunks.

4. Mash canned fish and gently spread it over the boiled chunky potatoes in a bowl and stir gently with a wooden

spoon. Sprinkle with pepper, salt and curry powder or nutmeg as needed.

5. Scoop enough mixture and place on the circular pastry.

6. Fold the mixture with the pastry to form a crescent or semi circle. Use fork to seal the semi circle. Continue this process with other circular pastry.

7. Place the pies in a pie pan and bake in a pre-heat oven temperature of 350 degrees. Bake for approximately 30 minutes.

Serve hot or cold with milk or any beverage.

BUNS

serves 6

RECIPE:

Flour	2 1bs
Baking powder	1 teaspoonful
Sugar	1/2 1b
Egg	6 eggs
Fresh milk	1 pint
Vegetable oil	1/4 pint.

METHOD:

(1) Mix flour and baking powder with fresh milk.

(2) Add sugar, eggs and vegetable oil.

(3) Mix thoroughly with a mixer to form a thick dough.

(4) Put the dough in a pie pan.

(5) Pre-heat an oven to a temperature of 350 degrees.

(6) Bake the dough for approximately 40-minutes.

Serve hot or cold with any beverage.

SCONES

serves 6

RECIPE:

Sugar	1/2 lb.
Fresh milk	2 quarts
Vegetable oil	as needed
Baking powder	1/2 teaspoonful
Flour	3 lbs.

METHOD:

(1) Mix flour and baking powder in a bowl containing milk.

(2) Add sugar, vegetable oil, and mix thoroughly in a mixer to form a thick dough.

(3) Flatten the dough to approximate thickness of one inch before cutting vertically and horizontally into small cubes. Place these cut dough in a pan and bake.

(4) Pre-heat an oven to a temperature of 350 degrees and bake for approximately 30-minutes.

PUFF PUFF

serves 6

RECIPE

Sugar	1lb.
Flour	3 1bs.
Yeast	2 tablespoonfuls
Palm juice	1 quart
Vegetable oil	as needed.
Water	one quart

METHOD:

(1) Dissolve sugar in a vessel containing approximate quantity of one quart of palm juice or two tablespoonfuls of yeast mixed with approximately 1 qt. of water.

(2) Mix the sugar, palm juice and flour in a mixer to form a thick consistency.

(3) Cover the dough in the vessel and place it on the sun or any other heat source until the dough rises.

(4) Then, roll the dough into small balls and fry in a deep skillet of oil.

Serve with any beverage.

CHIN CHIN

Serves 4

RECIPE:

Flour	3 1bs.
Baking powder	1/2 teaspoon

Nut meg	as needed
Sugar	2 lbs
Eggs	5 eggs
Milk	1/2 gal.

METHOD:

1. Thoroughly mix all ingredients:- flour, baking powder, eggs, sugar, milk, and nutmeg together.

2. Make dough into a big ball.

3. Use roller to evenly flatten the dough. Then, cut into tiny required shapes - triangular, circular or rectangular, as preferred.

4. Fry in a deep skillet of vegetable oil until brownish.

This is chin chin, a favourable snack.

Serve with any beverage.

FRUIT DESSERTS

RECIPE:

Use equal quantity of the following fruits cut into small pieces

Paw paw (papaya)	1/2 lb.
Pineapple	1/2 lb.
Orange	1/2 lb.
Banana	1/2 lb.
Apple	1/2 lb.
Cherries	1/2 lb.

Guava   1/2 lb.

Mix well in a bowl and serve.

UGBAKALA

(oil bean seed salad)

serves 6

RECIPE

Fermented oil bean seeds -- processed   1/2 lb

Ukazi leaf -- fresh -- cut   1 lb

Potash -- ground -- as needed or   1 teaspoonful

Palm oil   1/4 pint

Salt and pepper   as needed

Garden eggs -- sliced   10 large

Cray fish   1/2 oz

METHOD

1. Ground sauce is prepared by mixing potash, cray fish, palm oil, salt and pepper in the correct proportion with a little quantity of water of approximately 1/4 pint until a thick creamy orange color is formed. This is a dressing for salad.

2. Mix this dressing with the ukazi, garden eggs and the fermented oil beans and serve with any drink.

UKAZI SALAD

serves 3

<u>RECIPE</u>

Fresh ukazi leaf -- cut	1 lb
Vegetable oil or palm oil	as needed
Pepper --- ground	to taste
Potash -- ground	1/2 oz
Cray fish --- ground	1/2 oz

<u>METHOD</u>

Make sauce similar to that made with isi ewu (goat's head or ugbakala).

1. Put palm or vegetable oil in a bowl.
2. Add ground cray fish, ground potash, salt and pepper as needed. Stir to a proper consistency. This is a dressing for salad.
3. Mix this dressing with the ukazi.

Serve with palm juice or any beverage.

BANANA FRITTERS

serves 3

<u>RECIPE</u>:

Bananas	3 large ones
Flour	1 lb
Sugar	to taste
Milk	as needed

Baking powder	1/4 tea spoonful
Oil	as needed
Nutmeg	as needed
Eggs	2 eggs

METHOD:

(1)Thoroughly mash bananas and mix with flour, nutmeg, baking powder, sugar and milk to form a soft dough.

(2)Scoop a small quantity approximately one or two inches in diameter at a time with a spoon and fry in a skillet containing vegetable oil until it turns brownish.

KULIKULI

(peanut cake)

serves 5

RECIPE:

| Roasted peanuts | 3 lbs |
| Vegetable oil | as needed |

METHOD:

(1)Blend peanuts in a blender.

(2)Put the blended peanuts on a flat tray. Shape into a big ball. Squeeze and knead the ball to extract oil. Add worm water after each sqeeze to aid in the oil extraction. Repeat this procedure until all the oil has been extracted.

(3)Shape the large almost oil free peanut ball into small balls.

(4) Heat vegetable oil in a skillet. Fry slices of onions in the skillet for flavor. Then, fry the peanut balls until brownish. These are peanut cakes.

It can be served hot or cold.

COCONUT TOFFEE

serves 6

RECIPE:

Coconut milk	2 lbs.
Sugar	6 lbs.
Lemon juice	as needed

METHOD:

1. Prepare coconut milk or purchase two cans in your African food store.

2. Add sugar and lemon as needed . Stir continuosly until content turns brownish.

3. Reduce heat, and pour content into a greased pie pan and cut immediately into sections before it cools.

4. Allow to cool. It is now hardened and ready to be served.

PLAIN COCONUT BISCUIT

serves 5

RECIPE:

Flour	2 lbs
Coconut -- grated	1 lb
Sugar	1 lb
Margarine	1 lb
Eggs	4 eggs
Water --	as needed

METHOD

1.Mix sugar, eggs, flour and margarine into a light dough.

2.With a roller, roll dough in an evenly uniform thickness.

3.Put dough into a greased pie pan and bake in an oven at a temperature of 300 degrees for approximately 30 minutes or until brownish.

Serve with fresh milk or any beverage.

PEANUT BISCUIT

serves 10

RECIPE:

Peanuts -- chopped	2 lbs
Sugar	I lb
Eggs	6 eggs
Flour	4 lbs
Oil -- margarine or butter	1 lb

METHOD:

1)Blend sugar and margarine together to form a thick cream.

2.Add flour, chopped peanuts together and mix into a soft smooth dough.

3.Flatten with a roller to a thickness of approximately 1/2 inch. Cut into round biscuit size using a tumbler rim.

4.Bake in a pre-heat oven temperature of approximately 350 degrees for 30 minutes.

Serve with fresh milk or any beverage.

PLAIN CAKE

serves 5

RECIPE

Eggs	6 eggs
Flour	2 lbs
Sugar	1 lb
Baking soda	1 teaspoon
Milk	as needed
Margarine or butter	1 lb

METHOD:

1. Blend margarine or butter with flour, milk, sugar, baking powder to form a soft battar.

2. Pour into a greased baking pan and bake in an oven at 350 degrees for approximately 45 minutes.

Raymond Essang

EGG CUSTARD

serves 4

RECIPE

Eggs	10 eggs
Milk	as needed
Sugar	1 lb

METHOD

1. Heat milk on a stove.

2. Mix eggs with the boiled milk and stir.

3. Pour the content into a greased pie pan and bake in an oven at 300 degrees for approximately 60 minutes or bake until set.

CORN STARCH CUSTARD

RECIPE

Corn flour	1lb
Milk	1 lb
Sugar	¼ lb
Vanilla	1 tsp.

METHOD

1. Mix the corn flour, sugar ,milk vanilla together to a proper consistency.

2. Heat some portion of the milk and pour it over the corn mixture.

3. Cook with a medium heat for 5 minutes and stirring constantly until it boils.

4. Stir in the vanilla.

The corn starch is now ready.

DRINKING GARRI WITH ROASTED SHRIMP KEBUB

Garri as we had already known is a fried grated cassava. Garri can be drunk with roasted meat or roasted fish and sometimes with fresh coconut.

GURUDI

(starch coconut biscuit)

serves 3

RECIPE:

Cassava starch	1 lb
Coconut -- grated	2 lbs
Salt -- optional	as needed
Sugar	to taste
Water	as needed

METHOD:

1. Mix the above ingredients; starch, grated coconut, water, sugar and salt together to form a thin batter

2. Pour content into a greased pie pan and bake in an oven at 350 degrees for approximately 30 minutes.

3.Remove from the oven and cut into small squares with a knife.

4.Put the cut squares back into the oven and bake for additional 15 minutes.

5.Take it out and let it cool. Gurudi is now ready to be served with any drink.

SPONGE CAKE

serves 4

RECIPE:

Flour	2 lbs
Sugar	1 lb
Eggs	3 eggs
Milk	as needed
Baking powder	1/2 tea spoon

METHOD:

1.Thoroughly mix flour, eggs, sugar and baking powder with milk. Work into a thick batter.

2.Pour the batter into a greased baking pan and bake at 300 degrees for approximately 45 minutes.

Serve with any beverage.

OGEDE MIMI

Ingredients:

Bananas	3 bananas
Corn flour	1lb
Vegetable oil	1lb
Milk	enough
Sugar	1lb as needed

1. Crush or marsh the three bananas with a spoon.
2. Mix the corn flour, the nut meg and crush bananas to a proper consistency.
3. Fry in the vegetable oil for a few minutes

COCONUT PEANUT BUISCUITS

Ingredients:

Peanut butter	½ lb
Coconut [grated]	1lb
Wheat flour	2lbs
Salt -------	as needed
Margarine or butter	as needed
Eggs	5 eggs
Soda bicarbonate of Soda	
Sugar ---	as needed

METHOD

1.Mix all the above ingredients properly to form a stiff paste.

2. Roll it into a thin big flat shape. Then using a knife cut it into small shapes place in the bake pan and bake at 400F until golden.

3.The biscuit is now ready as it is now crispy to be eaten.

DOUGHNUT BALLS

Ingredients:

Wheat flour	3lbs
Palm wine	1lb
Eggs	5 eggs
Sugar--	as needed
Nutmeg --	as needed

METHOD

1.Dissolve in the fresh palm wine .Add flour and work the mixture into a thick consistency.

2.Add the eggs, nutmeg and then keep the dough for about 2 hrs.as to increase in size.

3.Then using a spoon , cut the dough. Then fry it in a deep pot of oil until golden.

Served with tea or coffee.

CARROT CAKE

Ingredients:

Wheat flour	2lbs
Carrot grated	2lbs
Lemon juice	2 tsp
Cinnamon	1tsp
Salt	as needed
Eggs	5 eggs
Sugar	½ lb
Margarine	1/2lb
Baking powder	3tsp

METHOD

1. Mix together all the above ingredients---sugar, margarine, eggs, and lemon to a proper consistency.
2. Then mix in the flour, cinnamon and the baking powder to form a workable dough.
3. Cut the dough into small balls of about 2 ins in diameter.
4. Insert into the ball some grated carrot.
5. Arrange these properly into a baking pan and bake at the temperature of 400F for 40 min or until golden.

OAT BUSCUIT

Ingredients

Whole meal flour	2 lbs
Margarine	enough
Brown sugar	1/4 lb
Salt	as needed

METHOD

1. Mix the above ingredients properly. Roll it flat and place in a baking pan which had been rubbed with oil.

2. Bake it at the oven temperature of 350F for about 30 mins.The biscuit is now dry and crispy .You can now put it in an airtight container.

GARRI BUSCUITS

Ingredients

Garri	sieved 1 lbs
Margarine	1/2 lb
Eggs	4 eggs
Sugar	1/4 lb
Baking powder and the bicarbonate of soda	
Wheat flour	2lbs
Lemon or orange juice ----	enough

METHOD

1. Mix all of the above ingredients together and work it in a stiff paste. Sieve the garri into a fine powder.

2.Roll out and cut into shapes--- square,round,triangles and then bake in an oven temperature of 400F until golden.

3.Your crispy biscuit is now ready.

MAIZE BALL

(owowo)

Ingredients

Raw peanut	1 lb
Coconut	½ lb
Milk or water	[just enough]
Dry corn	½ lb
Salt	to taste
Cow peas	1 lb
Bouillon cubes	5 cubes

METHOD

Corn can be used fresh or dry. If dried ,soak it overnight in a refrigerator It is not necessary to soak fresh corn.

1. Boil the corn for 45 minutes and then add the cowpeas and continue boiling for another 45 minutes.

2. Make sure that you keep putting water as it dries out.

3. Add the pea nuts, salt, bouillon cubes and cook for another 45 minutes.

4. Your owowo is now ready after you drain off the excess water and is served with coconut.

BANANA CAKE

Ingredients

Bananas	5 bananas
Eggs	4
Wheat flour	as needed
Butter	as needed
Baking powder	1 table spoonful

METHOD

1. Mix thoroughly the butter ,sugar, and flour and the baking powder and the raw eggs.
2. Mash the bananas and blend it thoroughly and consistently with the mixture to form a thick dough.
3. Bake in the baking pan at the temperature of 400F for 24 to 30 minutes until golden.

Serve with tea or coffee.

FREJON WITH MEAT

Ingredients

Black eye peas	2 lb
Fresh tomatoes sliced	3 medium
Coco nut milk	two cans
Fresh pepper	to taste
Beef, tripe or pork cut in chunks	

METHOD

1. Boil the beans until soft.

2. Cut the beef, pork and tripe in chunks and boil until tender.

2. Add the fresh tomatoes, onion, to the beans.

4. Season with the accent and the coconut milk to the mixture. Stir. Cook uncovered for 25 minutes until thickened.

5. Then add the cooked meat and stir.

Served with eba, pounded yam rice or boiled yam.

FREJON

<u>Ingredients</u>

Beans--- dark brown	2 lbs
Coco nut milk --	1 can
Sugar	to taste
Cloves	4

<u>METHOD</u>

1. Boil the black eye peas beans until soft.

2. Mash it into the paste with a wooden spoon or blender to produce a puree.

3. Add the coco nut milk and cloves to the mushy beans.

4. Boil uncovered and stir for 90 minutes until thick. Add a little sugar and salt to taste. The consistency should be creamy.

Serve with stew.

COOKED GROUND RICE

[Abala]

Ingredients

Rice flour	3 lbs
Salt and pepper	to taste
Onion [chopped]	2 medium
Fish [cut in chunks]	3
Palm oil	½ pint

METHOD

Into the pot of boiling water add onion, pepper and salt.

2. Add the rice flour slowly while stirring until smooth.

3. Add more water if necessary to produce a thick dropping consistency.

4. Scoop a little portion at a time into aluminum foil and wrap.

5. Allow it to cool before unwrapping and eating.

Can be eaten on its own or with stew.

CHUK CHUK

[Coco nut biscuits]

Ingredients

Eggs	4 eggs
Sugar	1lb
Flour as needed	2lbs
Coco nut [grated]	2 coco nuts

<u>METHOD</u>

1. Mix the grated coco nut with eggs and sugar to a proper consistency. Squeeze out a little coco nut water if it is too watery.

2. Mole it into small balls of about an inch in diameter and role each ball in the flour. You can cut it in small squares triangular or any other style you like.

4. Rub the aluminum foil with oil and place the balls on the aluminum foil.

5. Bake at the temperature of 400F until golden.

6. Chuk Chuk is now ready.

RICE AND PLANTAIN CAKE

<u>RECIPE</u>

Rice [soft boil]	3lbs
Eggs	4eggs
Vanilla	1tsp
Milk	as needed
Margarine	as needed
Wheat flour	1lb
Sugar	to taste

<u>METHOD</u>

Mix eggs with sugar and margarine properly.

1.Mix the remainder ingredients----milk, vanilla, flour, ripe plantain properly to form a suitable dough. You can either use a mixer or blender for the job.

2. Cut the dough into small sizes and bake at a oven temperature of 400F for 2hrs until brown.

Served with tea or coffee for break fast.

ROASTED CORN ON THE COB

In fact, roasting corn on the cob is one of the best way of eating corn since all the vitamins content are conserved. This can be achieved by peeling corn and baking it in the oven.

So also you can bake other foodstuffs like yam, cocoyam, plantain in the similar manner.

RICE PORRIDGE

RECIPE

Coconut	2lbs
Sugar	to taste
Rice	1lb

METHOD

1.Grind the coco nut in a blender and add a little water to make milk out of it. Flavor with vanilla or nutmeg

2. Boil the rice with milk until soft. Sprinkle sugar and serve.

DRINKS

PINEAPPLE DRINK

<u>RECIPE</u>:

Pineapple	1 large size
Water	1 gallon
Sugar	as needed

<u>METHOD</u>:

1. Peel pineapple and blend in a blender.
2. Add water and let sit for 4 hours.
3. Filter out the residue, add sugar as needed and drink.

GINGER DRINK

<u>RECIPE</u>:

Root ginger	9 roots
Water	1/2 gallon
Sugar	as needed

<u>METHOD</u>:

1. Peel and grind ginger root.
2. Add hot water and sugar. Let it stay overnight.
3. Filter and drink.

PLANTAIN DRINK

METHOD

1. Allow the plantain to be used to be fully ripe and soft.

2. Peel the plantain and cut or slice it in pieces. Add enough water as needed. You may wish to blend in a blender.

3. Allow it to sit over night in a refrigerator. Add a little sugar if necessary, it could be presumed that the banana sweetness alone will do.

Filter and drink.

ORANGE DRINK

RECIPE:

Oranges	12 oranges
Water	1 gallon
Sugar	as needed

METHOD

1.Peel oranges and squeeze out the juice.

2.Mix the juice with water and leave for 2-hours.

3.Filter, add sugar and drink.

LEMON DRINK

RECIPE

Lemons	10 lemons
Water	1/2 gallon
Sugar	as needed

METHOD

1. Cut lemons in halves and squeeze out juice.

2. Mix the juice with water and let sit for 2 hours.

3. Filter, add sugar as needed and serve.

GRAPE DRINK

RECIPE

Grapes	5 grapes
Water	1/2 gallon
Sugar	to taste

METHOD

1. Peel grapes and squeeze out juice.

2. Mix the juice with water and let sit for 2 hours.

3. Filter, add sugar and drink.

CONCLUSION

This cook book is unique in the sense that it is the first African cook book written by an African native, and published in the United States. The author uses authentic recipes in the preparation of each meal. Most of these African foods are medicinal, high in fibers, carbohydrates, iron, protein, and minerals. In essence, African foods are very good for those with adverse health conditions like high blood pressure, cancer, obesity, anemia and impotency.

It has been proven that Africans have stronger teeth as a result of their diet. Africans are more immune to contagious diseases. The reasons are obvious. It is the African diet. In addition to the health benefit of African diet, it is also very palatable.

Because the author is health conscious he discourages the use of alcoholic beverages, tea or coffee. Various tests conducted in the United States and abroad have confirmed without a doubt that alcohol, tea or coffee is not good for the body. They increase high blood pressure, cause nervousness and in higher quantity they cause tremor.

If African foods are prepared with the original recipes as outlined by the author, improvement in an individual's holistic health can be achieved. Scientific experiments discover that God uses all the 106 chemical elements found in nature to create man. A man longevity can be determined according to his ability to eat food containing these elements in a correct proportion. That is why it is necessary to eat various kinds of foods from other lands or cultures.

The reason Adam, Eve and Methuselah lived so long with good health was because they were able to make use of these elements in their diet in a proper proportion .

Incorporation of African foods with that of American foods can approach this proportion intake in man's body. This means longevity and good health.

Some of the elements are iodine, calcium, carbon, iron, copper, magnesium, uranium, oxygen, fluorine, chlorine, silver, hydrogen, potassium, nitrogen, sodium and zinc, just to mention a few. All taken in a correct proportion. They can be found in different kinds of fruits, leaves, seeds, fishes, animals, birds, herbs or even taken directly from nature like sodium chloride, potash or oxygen.

To stay healthy eat African heritage food and keep the legacy alive.

GLOSSARY

AROSIDOSI	Rice porridge
ABAK	Palm fruit pulp
ABAK	Another name for banga
AKANWU	Potash
ADUN	Corn ball porridge
AFANG	A kind of vegetable
AFIA	White
AGBONO	African bush mango seeds
AKAMU	Corn starch pulp
AKARA	Bean cake
ALAPA	Stew
ASA IWA	Grated cassava porridge
ASARO	Yam pottage
ASARO	Stew
ATAMA	A kind of vegetable
AYIBILIYI	Mixed boiled corn, beans & peanuts
BANGA	Palm fruit creme
BOLI	Baked plantain
BEJU	CASSAVA BUISCUITS
CHUK CHUK	coconut biscuits
CONGO MEAT	Snail
DODO	Fried plantain (ripe)
EBIGHE	A kind of yam

EBOT	Goat
EDIKANG IKONG	Fried vegetable soup
EDITA IWA	Cassava snack
EFERE	Soup
EFERE IBOKPOT	Corn soup
EFO	Any green vegetable
EGUSI	Mellon seeds
EKOKI	Wrapped ground corn
EKPANG	General name for wrapped grated food
EKPANG IWA	Wrapped grated cassava
EKPANG NKPONG	Wrapped grated cocoyam
ETIDOT	Bitter leaf
EWA	Beans
EWEDU	Slimy green vegetable
FOO-FOO	Any edible dough that can be eaten with soup.
FURAR	Rice
GUMBO	Big chunk okra
GARRI	Grated fried cassava
GBEGIRI	Bean stew
GERO	Millet
GUMBO	Chunk okra soup
GURUDI	Starch coconut biscuit
IBABA	A kind of edible seeds
IKON	Mellon seeds

IKOKORE	Grated cocoyam balls
ILA	Okra
IRU	Locust beans
ISI EWU	Goat Head
IWUK UKOM	Sliced plantain porridge
IYAN	Pounded yam or coco yams
KELEWELE	Chunk fried plantains
KULI KULI	Peanut cake
NWUP	Mixed vegetable soup
MOYIN MOYIN	Bean pie
NGWO NGWO	Pepper soup made of animal parts.
NKUKWO	Young cocoyam leaf
NSOKOBI	Delicatessen
OGI	Corn starch
OJOJO	Fried grated water yam
OTO	Grated water-yam porridge
OTONG	A kind of slimy potash okra soup
OWO	A kind of potash soup
SUYA	Roasted beef
TUWO CHINKAFA	Rice foo-foo
UGBAKALA	Fermented African oil bean seeds
UKAZI	A kind of vegetable
UKWUOHO	Dry fry soup
USUNG	Another name for foo-foo
UTASI	A kind of leaf bitter in taste

UYAYAK   Long wing beans use for flavoring

ABOUT THE AUTHOR

Mr. Raymond Essang, the author of this book was a restaurant owner in Nigeria who managed and operated his restaurant. It was during the time of his entrepreneurship that he developed experience and interest in preparing African foods. Due to the increased demand for health foods by Americans, he decided to write this cook book.

He is also an engineering graduate from North Carolina A&T State University.

I admire his zeal and ingenuity for having broken the ice in writing the first West African Heritage Cook Book which is going to be the symbol of African heritage foods in the United States, thus enlightening the world about what our fore mothers left for us. He also has to be recommended for his love and thought about this important aspect of African culture.

Mr. Peter Archibong

CPSIA information can be obtained at www.ICGtesting.com
Printed in the USA
BVOW05s0658190714

359753BV00001B/28/A

9 781420 859966